CANADA

PRIME MINISTER • PREMIER MINISTRE

Dear Publisher,

I yam as Prime Minister of hall Canadian very 'appy to be hable to take dis time to sign dis letter which 'ave been type up and hon my desk for me to do so.

Ottawa is da name we in'erit from da first peoples dat mean 'dose dat 'ave hears'. Or 'dealer'. Or 'people in da wood'. Somet'ing like dat. We are not sure which one 'old up in court, but we work id out togedder. First, we 'ave ear to listen to da people when dey speak to us. And den sometime we make deal, like wid da provinces over power and money. Or radder lack of it. And, not to be forgotten 'iding behind da odder two meaning, we yare still in da wood, and not yet find our way out to de odderside. So we yare hall dese t'ings, and more, to hall people.

I yam comfortable wid dat. And for dose who come to Ottawa to visit, or to do some workout wid da government and da law, den such a book as dis can honly be welcome, and maybe it 'ave almost as much laugh for dem in it as da Red Book do for us now.

We yare, I yam told, in da time for information. Information we share wid heach odder, and id 'elp us to see groat in our heconomy. Groat by little bit and little byte and megabyte and whatever kine of package dey come in. All flying halong da 'ighway, hamong da transport truck, da tourist, and da many Canadian going dis way and dat. Or even da printed page, like dis book. It too 'ave information in it. And who know, some go to various bookstore in a van or a truck or whatever halong da same 'ighway as heveryone else. Id is da type of t'ing we Liberals 'ave halways supported for our future. We want to be da government of hall Canadian, and if dis book can 'elp dem to hunderstand us, and explain why in Ottawa we do what id is we 'ave to do, and 'ow id is done, by whom and to whom, den I yam hall for it.

I yam proud to be a Canadian. I yam proud to 'elp Canadian learn habout dis great country, and to a lesser hextent, its government. We can hall be proud of dis guide, and hall Canadian publisher we 'ave manage to keep out of the 'ands of odder countries. I t'ank you, and wish you hevery good fortune wid dis project.

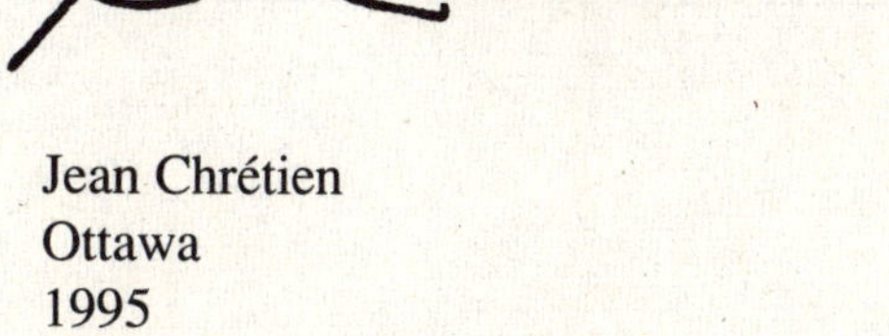

Jean Chrétien
Ottawa
1995

The following contains no similarity to any government living or dead, or any person living or dead. Or any cabinet minister living or dead, or still serving as Minister because the Prime Minister is foolishly unwilling to admit he made a real mistake in putting the guy there in the first place.

The following also contains no similarity to any national capital living or dead, or political party living or dead, or advice for personal growth, self-acceptance and happiness.

Frankland Capital Corporation accepts no responsibility, writs, or collect phone calls arising in a timely manner from the material in this book. Any similarity to any corporation real or imagined is unintended, though our accountants are working dilligently on creating this illusion before the hearing date.

Any wanton misappropriation of the material in this book for purposes unintended by the publisher will result in acutely embarrassing personal itches, increasing Bank of Canada prime lending rates, and the immediate return of Brian Mulroney to daily television.

For those still offended at not being included in this book by name, you may pencil it in here:

____ is a Great Canadian™.

(Offer void where prohibited by the lack of a writing tool. Not applicable to Pat McAdam.)

FRANK'S MILLENNIAL GUIDE TO OTTAWA

GEOFF HEINRICKS

KEY PORTER BOOKS

Canadian Catologuing in Publication Data

Heinricks, Geoffrey
Frank's millennial guide to Ottawa

ISBN 1-55013-708-5

1. Canada – Politics and government – Humor.
2. Ottawa (Ont.) – Humor. I. Title.

FC173.H45 1995 971.3'84 C95-931692-2

The publisher gratefully acknowledges the assistance of the Canada Council, the Ontario Arts Council and the Ontario Publishing Centre.

Key Porter Books
70 The Esplanade
Toronto, Ontario
Canada M5E 1R2

Printed and bound in Canada

95 96 97 98 99 5 4 3 2 1

CANADA

The Frank Guide to Ottawa Act

November 1995

Table of Contents

Forces Irresistible

2. a) Parliament Hill
   b) Privy Council
   c) Prime Minister's Office
   d) Cabinet
   e) The Bank of Canada
   f) The Supreme Court of Canada
   g) The Armed Forces
   h) Spooks

III
Non-Physical or Non-Theoretical Bipedal Elements of Structural Integrity and Infrastructure Modalities, Forces and Units affecting and effecting Governance, Sovereignty, and Monetary Exchange

1. a) The Liberal Party
   b) The Reform Party
   c) The Bloc Québécois
   d) The New Democratic Party
   e) The Progressive Conservative Party
   f) Independent Members of Parliament
   g) The Public Service
   h) Media

IV
Separate but Equal Quebec Section

a) The Question
b) The Answer

V
Miscellanea

a) Social Life in Ottawa

(enough with the fine print already, let's get on with it – ed.)

Overview and Synopsis

As October 25, 1993, drew closer, and it appeared the Liberals would return to power, there was a deep gloom over the central Canadian edition of *Frank* Magazine. Editor Michael Bate made it clear to those of us who drew sustenance from Frankland Capital that we were in for dire times. Almost five years of mirthful growth, directly attributable to the scourge of Brian Mulroney, had kept our Halifax directors and shareholders happy. Kim Campbell had been a decent replacement, if not in the Tories' view, then at least in *Frank*'s. But anytime Jean Chrétien got on or anywhere near the cover of an issue, everything crumbled. The fear of the Liberals returning to power under this guy caused many sleepless nights, cheerless conversations, and a quick liquidation of personal assets to ride out what promised to be a looming satirical drought.

Fortunately the show in Ottawa continues better than before. If we sat down as a group (which Franksters rarely get to do, instead working through fax, modem, telephone and bus parcels), I don't think we could have created what we now have in Reform. Lucien Bouchard and the Bloc were only the sound of one hand clapping until Jacques Parizeau became Premier of Quebec. Now Bouchard and Parizeau are slapping along like veteran vaudevillians, causing more laughter than consternation.

Even the Liberals have turned out better than expected. While Prime Minister Chrétien has all but taken up golf professionally, and miraculously holds at record levels in the polls, his party has already provided Jag Bhaduria, and some solidly substandard ministers. The delightful and highly visible internal feuds afflicting the party, as MPs try to wrestle with the shock of assuming Brian Muldoon's policies with an energy the Tories themselves never knew, show a cranky individuality the Tories also never knew. And that's good for leaks to *Frank*.

Ottawa itself has also changed. The flash and cheese of the Mulroney years has evaporated. And so has much of the high-end lobbying industry. The Liberals have exclusive fund-raising and access schemes like the Laurier Club, where $1,000 gets you in a room with Jean Chrétien, so who needs a third-party lobbyist when you have that, or David Dingwall's phone number, or someone at Power Corporation? O.K., not many people can boast of such contacts, but we all have the potential to. That's what Liberalism is all about. Liberals are hands-on governors, and aren't quite as cliquey or paranoid as the last bunch. They are accustomed to Ottawa, in a way most Canadians never can be.

So here's an inexpensive way to even the score. It won't help you navigate the ugly public art on the Sparks Street Mall. Nor will it push you through the corridors of power with enough verve to get a contract or boon the first time you try. But at least you'll know who and what these people and places are and what they're capable of. Which, in truth, is exactly what they don't want.

The Queen

The head of state in Canada is the Queen. The Queen of what? one may ask. Constitutionally, "HER MOST EXCELLENT MAJESTY ELIZABETH THE SECOND (Elizabeth Alexandra Mary of Windsor) by the Grace of God of the United Kingdom, Canada and Her other Realms and Territories Queen, Head of the Commonwealth, Defender of the Faith, Sovereign of the British Orders of Knighthood and Sovereign Head of the Order of Canada and of the Order of St. John, Captain General of the Royal Regiment of Artillery and the Honourable Artillery Company, Colonel-in-Chief of the Life Guards, the Royal Horse Guards, the Royal Scots Greys (and Dragoons), the 16th/5th the Queen's Royal Lancers, the Royal Tank Regiment, the Corps of Royal Engineers, the Grenadier Guards, the Coldstream Guards, the Scots Guards, the Irish Guards, the Welsh Guards, the Royal Welsh Fusiliers, the Loyal Regiment (N. Lancashire) and Green Jackets K.R.R.C., the Argyll and Sutherland Highlanders, Royal Malta Artillery R.A.O.C., Duke of Lancaster's Own Yeomanry, Hon. Colonel Queen's Own Warwickshire and Worcestershire Yeomanry, Captain-General Combined Cadet

Force, Captain-General Royal Regiment of Canadian Artillery, Colonel-in-Chief Corps of Royal Canadian Engineers, Royal 22nd Regiment, the Royal Canadian Ordnance Corps, the King's Own Calgary Regiment (RCAC), Governor General's Foot Guards, the Canadian Grenadier Guards, Le Régiment de la Chaudière, the Royal New Brunswick Regiment, 48th Highlanders of Canada and the Argyll & Sutherland Highlanders of Canada (Princess Louise's), Air Commodore-in-Chief R.C.A.F Auxiliary and Hon. Commissioner Royal Canadian Mounted Police®™."

Think of Liz as our collective safe-deposit box, since all power in the country ultimately rests with her, and is signed out by our elected politicians only until the next election. But as we share Betty Windsor with about fifty other nations, protectorates, devoluted colonies, and tax havens, we use her domestic stunt double known as the Governor General.

VISIT OF HER MAJESTY THE QUEEN

POST-REFERENDUM CEREMONY

Program

Monday, June 17, 1996

10:30 A.M.	***Her Majesty The Queen leaves Great Britain***
12:45 P.M.	***Her Majesty The Queen enters Canadian airspace***
12:46 P.M.	***Her Majesty The Queen waves***
12:50 P.M	***Her Majesty The Queen departs Canadian airspace***

The public is invited to participate.

Department of Foreign Affairs

Ministère des Affaires Art Eggleton

Canada

The Governor General

The Governor General is a highly partisan Canadian politician appointed on the increasingly wonky but binding advice of the Canadian Prime Minister, who then has a friend or former political flunkie around for about five years, throwing neat parties across the street from 24 Sussex. Despite the increasingly pungent ripeness of pig-blind hackery wafting about the Governors General appointed in the last 15 or 20 years, the choices are always excellent, and so the flunkie and his wife (shurly Sauvé mistake – ed.) are always known as "His and Her Excellencies." At least until they're replaced by the next pair of even more excellent Excellencies. And so on until enough wilful damage has finally been done to ensure the dismantling of our constitutional monarchy.

With the Senate and the Commons, the Queen makes up the trinity of parliamentary government in Canada. All laws are passed in her name, beginning with "Her Majesty, by and with the advice and consent of the Senate and the House of Commons, enacts as follows..." Parliament must be summoned by the Queen, or more commonly her stunt double, to carry on business. Bills become law only after receiving Royal Assent from one or the other, or an officially appointed official stand-in stunt double. After elections, the Governor General usually appoints as Prime Minister the leader of the party with the most asses on seats in the House of Commons. The Governor General then governs the country by acting on the advice of this new Prime Minister and Cabinet, who in turn are answerable to those financing their electoral success in putting the most asses on seats in the House of Commons.

I look forward to meeting many of you from across this young nation. We all have much to rejoice in. To celebrate. To learn.

As Governor General, my wife and I hope to share rejoicing, celebration and learning with you.

And the first lesson is for the kids who think I played Grampa on The Munsters. I didn't.

The governing combination of the Governor General and the Prime Minister and his ministers (privy councillors all) is called the Governor General-in-Council. It has a great degree of power and discretion in what it may do without consulting the Commons or Senate, mainly with senior appointments and administrative details. The Governor General has the right to be consulted by his ministers, and the right to encourage or warn them. But these rights are rarely, if ever, exercised now.

Most of the time Their Excellencies perform ceremonial duties, attend or run meet-and-greets, deal with the duller formalities of diplomacy, pass out gongs and honours, and behave themselves. Most have done just fine.

Rideau Hall and the grounds are rather spectacular. A drive around the perimeter, with the endless stone and iron fence, makes it clear something special lurks there. How best to keep it from becoming a joke is the problem.

The Constitution

According to the universally respected constitutional authority, the Right Honourable Martin Brian Muldoon, Canada's constitution "isn't worth the paper it's written on." That was his pronouncement in April 1989, and he spent the rest of his time in government doing everything in his power to win people over to his side. With his sly Irish charm and silver tongue, it almost worked.

The cause of Mulroney's whine is the fact that Pierre Trudeau has credit for a constitution in the history books, while Muldoon – a far greater man than the obsessively despised Trudeau – does not. Over an Ontario of felled pulpwood and a Lake Erie of used videotape, the winds of constitutional desolation still faintly, drily whisper "Meech Lake" and "Charlottetown," but only in *Globe and Mail* columns. The Constitution, the hearty forage of Canadian pundits, consultants, and lobbyists for decades, has failed them over the past few years. However, Muldoon did have one constitutional success few know of. In 1988 he secured the patriation of the Queen's power over heraldry to the Governor General. Six years later, in December 1994, both he and Trudeau, patriators of a small and large bit of our constitution, were granted coats of arms within days of each other. Though Trudeau, damn him, got his first.

The major piece of legal work making up our constitution is the British North America Act, 1867. It is now called the Constitution Act, 1867, and was the result of various conferences held to work out an agreement to unite and self-govern Ontario, Quebec, New Brunswick, and Nova Scotia. The new entity was called the Dominion of Canada. Since 1867, and like the ball of string called the Common Law, the Constitution has grown to encompass a few dozen British and Canadian orders-in-council and acts of Parliament. Until 1982 these various parts of the Constitution set up a federal state, the provinces and the territories, and a federal Parliament and provincial legislatures, defining their powers; vested executive power in the Queen and created the Queen's Privy Council for Canada; allowed Parliament to create a Supreme Court; and guaranteed Quebec (and other provinces) certain religious, linguistic, and legal rights. Any changes required British legislation.

In 1982, after many years of brilliantly maintained economic failure, Trudeau finally redirected Canada's attention from unemployment and inflation to the Constitution. A workable deal was reached to sever legislative ties with the British Parliament, and settle the mess of constitutional documents – and procedures to create further documents – solely in Canada. The Constitution Act, 1982, renamed some of the old bits of the Dadaist creation, and pruned a bit off the others, but essentially it wasn't a new constitution we got, but a repositioning exercise on the one we've always had. However, there were a few new elements to the thing, chiefly: amending formulas for future changes; a Charter of Rights and Freedoms (home of the delightful "notwithstanding clause" that negates any of the rights Parliament or a legislature finds inconvenient for five-year stretches); and granting the provinces increased control over their natural resources. Tacking close to the legal breeze, but without a hope of unanimity with the PQ running Quebec, enough people were happy with the thing. Betty Windsor flew in to finalize the paperwork in April 1982. (Trudeau allowed Jean Chrétien to sign the document as well, though his signature has all the legal force and necessity of an autograph in a high-school yearbook.) And Poof! a huge new area of specialization and growth was created for our lawyers.

Most of the working elements of our government, from the public service to the Prime Minister, Cabinet, and even Parliament, are the result of legislation, custom, or court judgement. They don't exist constitutionally, or only in passing. Few people realize how important custom is to the

Out of the way! Power minister coming through. Look out, sister

Savour it, honey. Don't be in such a rash to get out the door.

Believe me, you'll be there soon enough once the boys tire of you. Wait and see.

operation of government in Canada. One of the strongest arguments for a muck-raking, disrespectful media and unruly opposition in the Commons is to watch those in government to ensure they're not dicking around with power, because so little of it is tidily organized in boxes of legal clause and subclause. It also requires a collective memory, something the media and opposition are neglecting through ignorance or laziness.

For People Who Don't Want to Read the First Five Paragraphs

For those who slept through the last 13 years of constitutional peril, or were spared it, here's a recap. Pierre Elliott Trudeau, after failing at previous attempts at constitutional patriation, used his promise to Quebec during the 1980 referendum to renew federalism to try again. With Chrétien and other political and public service lawyers turned loose, general agreement was reached to patriate and amend the Constitution. Quebec, represented by sovereignty-associationist René Lévesque, was frozen out, and did not sign. Which is not surprising. Lévesque agreeing to sign was about as likely as Svend Robinson being asked to edit the *ROB*. But since the federal government was led and dominated by Quebecers, nobody felt too bad.

The exception was a Tory back-room weasel named Brian Mulroney. Whispering and lying his way to the Prime Minister's Office, Muldoon hearkened to his old chum Lucien Bouchard, and to his premier René Lévesque, that the Constitution was not a worthy document until Quebec signed. And for Quebec to sign, a shifting dune of minimum demands had to be met. The Meech Lake Accord was fashioned to meet most of these. When the time limit set up in the Constitution's amending formula was reached before ratification, in great part because of political gamesmanship, the amendment package died. Mulroney then tried again, and this time all the provinces, including Quebec, piled on with special constitutional requests, and the Charlottetown agreement was born. This time it was put to a national referendum, and soundly turned down by people in and out of Quebec.

Er, that's it.

Parliament Hill

The majestic collection of stone buildings atop Barrack Hill, 150 feet above the Ottawa River, houses Canada's legislators and serves as an attractive backdrop for television reporters and protesters. And also in typical Canadian fashion, they sit on part of a 3.4 million-hectare land claim by Algonquin natives from the Golden Lake reserve. (The band argues that the Crown signed a treaty in 1819 with Mississauga Indians but not with Algonquins. Not surprisingly, Quebec Algonquins also claim the same territory. The Golden Lake reserve has offered to lease or sell back the land at market value, but so far the government hasn't taken them up on the offer.)

There are three main buildings on the Hill, huddled around the Centennial flame for warmth, all in a style referred to as neo-Gothic. The original green slate roofs were replaced decades ago with copper at the order of self-taught architect and spiritualist Mackenzie King, who instinctively rearranged the face of Ottawa to reflect corporate interests or fashions, particularly the Château Laurier.

At the centre-front of the main or Centre Block is the shrouded Peace Tower, wrapped in sheeting and scaffolding in what will be a long restoration of the building. At the centre-rear is the majestic, round Parliamentary Library. The rest of the building contains the Senate (or Red) Chamber, the House of Commons (or Green) Chamber, committee meeting rooms, public space, the Prime Minister's photo-op office, the Cabinet room, and about two floors of offices for Members of Parliament. On the sixth floor is an elaborate and elegant dining room that will be pressed into service as the Green Chamber after the millennium because of future renovations to the building.

The East Block is the oldest building on the Hill, and once provided space for the Prime Minister, Cabinet, and the Privy Council. Now it mainly serves as museum and nursing home for senators. The West Block provides more office space and meeting and support rooms, and contains a large cafeteria.

The original Centre Block burned down on February 3, 1916. The fire was blamed on Germans who obviously wanted to get in a little early practice before torching the Reichstag. Seven people perished in the blaze. Most accounts claim it started in the Reading Room, and, with this in mind, almost 75 years later the Tories gutted the new Centre Block Reading Room, removed the fire hazard, and turned it into another regular committee room, but one that was often pressed into service as a classy backdrop for many of Muldoon's Theatre of the Absurd press conferences and ceremonies.

Not many people know that burning down Parliament is something of a minor Canadian pastime. On April 25, 1849, a Montreal mob torched the then Canadian Houses of Assembly because of the passage of the Rebellion Losses Bill, making today's Canadian gun lobby and maverick Liberal backbenchers look like weenies. No group has yet claimed responsibility for the 1916 blaze, but if Health Minister Diane Marleau was as smart as she looked, she'd turn it into the centrepiece of her anti-smoking campaign. For the future, Canada certainly boasts pyro bench-strength when one casts a wary eye over both Reform and German history between the wars.

The Senate

The Upper or Red Chamber, located on the right side of the Centre Block, was constructed as a more democratic House of Lords, and functions

PERIODIC TABLE OF SENATORS

87 **Richard Dawson*** BC	69		Throne Speaker **Gildas Molgat** MN		17 **Julius Robert Ottenheimer** NF	35 **Duncan Justaman** MN
88 **Michael Outfield*** ON	70 **Dead Wood** QU	Liberal Orbit			18 **Tom Cochrane** NF	36 **Leonard Gustafson** SK
89 **Keith Davey-Clark-Five** ON	71 **Leo Kolbassa** QU	53 **Louis Riel** QU	Clerk	1 **John Eh Macdonald** NS	19 **René Simard** NB	37 **J. Michael Fox** NS
90 **Michael Kirby** CTV	72 **Lucky Lucier** YU	54 **Earl of Hastings** AB		2 **Anne Murray** ON	20 **Consiglio El Nino** ON	38 **Ian & Sylvia** QU
91 **Lord Thompson** ON	73 **Strawberry Risotto** QU	55 **Stanbury Connecticut** BC	Clerk Assistant	3 **Guy Charbonneau** QU	21 **Louise Beaudoin** QU	39 **Normand Dee** QU
92 **Corbin Bernsen** NB	74 **Gerry Raftstream** ON	56 **Austin City Limits** BC		4 **Lloyd Robertson** NB	22 **Eileen Cosset** PEI	40 **Janis Joplin** MN
93 **George S. Petten** NF	75 **Neiman Marcus** ON	57 **Jimmy Olson** AB		5 **Chili Con Carney** BC	23 **Roch Boulder** QU	41 **Very Meighen** ON
94 **Avi Lewis** NF	76 **James Lovell** PEI	58 **Ellen MacEachen** NS		6 **Pat Buchanan** NS	24 **Mabel Black Label** NB	42 **Davie Keon** ON
95 **Patrick Stewart** NS	77 **Philippe Gigantès** QU	59 **Joyce Fairbairn** AB	Official Reporters	7 **John Lynch-Pynn** QU	25 **W.P. Kinsella** NB	43 **Suwannee Rivest** QU
96 **Kenny Rodgers** ON	78 **Anne Hébert** QU	60 **Billy Graham** NS		8 **Bernston Bears** SK	26 **Dickie Doyle** ON	44 **Rayon Audreychuk** SK
97 **Stollery Parkette** ON	79 **Bosa Nova** ON	61 **Charles Perrault** BC		9 **Howdy Doody** NF	27 **Craig Oliver** NS	45 **Terrance Stratton** MN
98 **Bobbie Sparrow** SK	80 **Brian Adams** NWT	62 **Luc Robichaud** NB		10 **Michelle Phillips** PEI	28 **Normal Atkins** ON	46 **Pinch Ghitter** AB
99 **Abbé Groulx** QU	81 **Forty Watt** QU	63 **Stanley Häagen-Dazs** ON		11 **DeForest Kelley** ON	29 **Therèse La-Vie-en-Rose** QU	47 **Leonard Cohen** NB
100 **Back Bacon** QU	82 **Cool Hand-Luke** ON	64 **Novel Theory** QU	Official Reporters	12 **Ronald McDonald's** NS	30 **Mila Sputnik** MN	48 **Fernand Auberge** QU
101 **Joan Bryden** SOUTHAM	83 **Michel Gauthier** ON	65 **Jean Marchand** BC		13 **James Taylor** ON	31 **Michel Robber** QU	49 **Terry Sawchuk** SK
102 **Pearson International** ON	84 **Carstairs Upstairs** MN	66 **Pierre Dubonnet** QU		14 **Balfour Take a Base** SK	32 **Baie Comeau** NS	50 **Black Angus** QU
103	85 **Lose Your-Cool*** NB	67 **Gabby Hays** AB	Gentleman Usher of the Black Rod	15 **Gerry & the Pacemakers** BC	33 **Patrick Twinn-Cité** AB	51 **Non Demarais** ON
104 **Nolin Ryan** ON	86	68 **Hervé Villachez** QU	OPEN BAR	16 **Marcel Prud'homme*** QU	34 **Never Eaton** ON	52 **LeBreton Flats** ON

• Free Radical

as the Chamber of Sober, Second Thought™. But as a Toronto hairstyling shop on Yonge Street already had a claim on the name "House of Lords," the Fathers of Confederation were forced to pinch the name of a gormless Ottawa pro hockey team – The Senators. Currently 101 strong, these ersatz Senators are appointed on merit, as determined by the governing political party of the day, and serve until they reach 75 or the odour becomes noticeable and a reputable funeral home is summoned. Landing a Senate appointment is good for $64,000 a year plus a $10,000 tax-free allowance. As Tory apologist Hugh Segal says every chance he gets, "The Senate is a taskless thanks."

The senators, because they're appointed, usually lag about one election behind in party representation. That means the political party forming the government can often find itself with a Senate packed with members of an opposing party and thus outvoted. This potential to harass the government of the day is often the only reason the majority of senators have to get out of bed every day.

The Speaker of the Senate is appointed by the Queen's stunt double on the advice of Cabinet and, like his counterpart in the House of Commons, has administrative powers in addition to keeping senators awake and at work approving the bits and pieces of the government's legislation that catch their fancy. (The ability to hold up most of the bills passed onto it by the Commons is the Senate's one remaining vital sign, since the lack of television cameras in the Chamber gives it the profile and impact of an unattended tree tumbling in a forest.) The Speaker is aided in overseeing the Senate by a few clerks, and by Black Rod, Canada's answer to Shaft, Superfly, and the other heroes of Afro-American exploitation films of the 1970s. More properly known as the Gentleman Usher of the Black Rod, he is the personal attendant to the representative of Her Majesty in the Senate. Armed only with an ebony rod topped with a gold lion, Black Rod serves as both messenger and shepherd for the trinity making up Parliament – the Sovereign or her stunt double, the Senate, and the House of Commons – whenever they have to get together at the opening or proroguing of Parliament or for Royal Assent to bills passed by both Houses. When not so occupied, Black Rod fights crime in the Centre Block, East Block, and Victoria Building with his own force of security guards, and arrests those with bad manners or threatening dispositions.

The House of Commons

The 295 elected representatives from across Canada can be found about 100 days a year in the House of Commons, which is located on

The Honourable Member for Rambling Wild Rose will pose a question or shut it.

(C'mon, Reform Boy, listen to what I told you!)

Supplemental? Yeah, I got your supplemental right here, Myron. Sit. The Honourable Member for Laurentides-Babeland.

the west side of the Centre Block. Well, maybe not actually in the Chamber, because for most of those 100 days there's barely a quorum. But they are often nearby, engaged in committee work, stuck in meetings with constituents or school groups, or quietly sobbing at the futility of their existence.

Lawyers still provide the bulk of MPs, or at least those destined for Cabinet. And the gender of choice is still male.

Until World War II, MPs had a fair degree of independence and influence in the House. And even respect among Canadians. Debates mattered, and were followed closely. But it was all lost to increasingly powerful prime ministers who found ways of beating their own members into strict obedience through party discipline, or more accurately the new bribes or punishments a modern prime minister could scatter about at will. And once the government benches were psychologically or financially beaten into submission, successive governments have pummelled the opposition into giving up the rights and traditional privileges of the House to oppose, challenge, and even block the government of the day from doing what it will. As a result, opposition in Parliament has become a loud, childish farce because it is relatively harmless, bordering precariously on pointless. Other than embarrassing the governing party with adverse media coverage snipped from sustained Question Period attacks and outrageous scrum comments in the foyer of the House of Commons, opposition members have more in common with government backbenchers than they and the backbenchers realize.

In charge of the show is the Speaker of the House of Commons, an MP elected at the start of each new Parliament. The Speaker maintains order in the House, rules on procedural disputes, and ensures each member can perform his or her elected role in physical or mental security. Three other MPs are also elected as stunt doubles for the Speaker, and get to dress up and sit on the big chair when the Speaker gets bored. The Speaker also holds neat parties, entertains in his own private dining room in the Centre Block and, with the Speaker of the Senate, pretty much controls the money and perks that pulse through the little fiefdom on Parliament Hill. In this he's helped by a handful of clerks and a sergeant-at-arms, whose ability to inflict misery on an MP through control of office space, services, and other perks earns them a child-like awe and fear.

Most of the important decisions about the financial and administrative policy of the House of Commons are taken by the Board of Internal Economy, whose almost limitless powers to run much of the Hill are wielded in near-secrecy. The Board is chaired by the Speaker, and consists of the Hourourable Gilbert Parent (Chairman), Don Boudria, Gilles Duceppe, Hon. Alfonso Gagliano, Michel Gauthier, Hon. Herb Gray, P.C., Len Hopkins, David Kilgour, and Bob Ringma.

The representation from all parties and Cabinet usually ensures that ridiculous or self-interested decisions or policies don't draw attention, since everyone had a hand in drafting them or at least agreed to them.

Since 1974 the House of Commons has endured television cameras in the Green Chamber, changing the dress and cleanliness of members for the better. The lack of anything useful to do in the Commons or in Committee (an average MP's likelihood of influencing a bill cobbled together by Cabinet and the Public Service is about as certain as Sir John A. Macdonald sweeping into power in 1998) has made getting on TV the only diversion. Whether it is only for the brief seconds an MP gets for statements just before Question Period, or the forlorn hope of being scrummed (or mocked, jostled, and robbed) by reporters in the foyer of the Commons after Question Period, it's what keeps MPs overlooked by party whips trooping into the Chamber.

Sad.

Hon. Members

Separating the Sheep from the Goats in the 35th House of Commons

When Pierre Trudeau snarled that members of the House of Commons were "nobodies" once they were 20 minutes from Parliament Hill, he got it wrong. It is mainly on Parliament Hill that the tiny, relatively useless and harmless mass of MPs wallow in their uselessness and lack of menace. Bullied when not ignored by their own political parties, and by bureaucrats and ministers, they're tiny people huddled near the curtains of House television coverage.

Most are led like sheep, shorn of dignity and the rightful independence and power they hoped would await them in Ottawa. Instead, a small handful of goats really run things in the Green Chamber and get the media's short attention. You can't tell the animals without a program. Here's the program.

Jim Abbott
Kootenay East Northwest
REFORM Sheep

Diane Ablonczy
Calgary North Centre West
REFORM Goat

Peter Adams
Peterborough
LIBERAL Sheep

Reg Alcock
Winnipeg South East Northwest
LIBERAL Sheep

Warren Allmand
Notre-Dame-de-Gracie-Allen
LIBERAL Sheep in Scapegoat's Clothing

Vic Althouse
Lewis-Mackenzie Delta
NDP Shorn Sheep

Jack Anawak
Nunatsiaq
LIBERAL Sheep

David Anderson
Victoria
LIBERAL Baaaaaa

Guy Arseneault
Restigouche-Chaleur
LIBERAL Sheep

Mark Assad
Gatineau-La Lièvre
LIBERAL Mutton

Sarkis Assadourian
Don Valley North Centre East
LIBERAL Sheep

Gérard Asselin
Charlevoix
BLOC Mouton

Jean Augustine
Etobicoke-Lakeshore-Slowdown on the Q.E.W.
LIBERAL Sheep

Chris Axworthy
Saskatoon Berry-Clark's Crossing
NDP Shorn Sheep

Lloyd Axworthy
Winnipeg South Centre-Ville
LIBERAL Scapegoat

Claude Bachand
Saint-Jean
BLOC Mouton

George Baker
Gander-Grand Falls
LIBERAL Lost Sheep

Eleni Bakopanos
Saint-Denis Moore
LIBERAL Rack of Lamb

Susan Barnes
London West
LIBERAL Ewe

Colleen Beaumier
Brampton
LIBERAL Baaaaaa

Réginald Bélair
Glen Cochrane-Superior
LIBERAL Sheep

Mauril Belanger
Ottawa-Vanier
LIBERAL Wooly Booly

Richard Bélisle
La Prairie
BLOC Mouton

Michel Bellehumeur
Berthier-Montcalm
BLOC Mouton

Eugène Bellemare
Carleton-Gloucester-Worcestershire Sauce
LIBERAL Three Bags Full

Leon Benoit
Vegreville
REFORM Sheep

Stéphane Bergeron
Verchères
BLOC Mouton

Maud Bergeron-Debien
Alea Jacta Est
BLOC Agneau

Gilles Bernier
Beauce
INDEPENDENT Brebis

Maurice Bernier
Magnetic-Compton-Bedstead
BLOC Mouton

Yvan Bernier
Gaspé
BLOC Mouton

Robert Bertrand
Pontiac-Gatineau-Patti Labelle
LIBERAL Mouton

Judy Bethel
Edmonton East North Centre
LIBERAL Ewe

Maurizio Bevilacqua
York North Southwest
LIBERAL Sheep

Jag Bhaduria
Markup-Witch Hunt-Stouffers
INDEPENDENT Goat in Black Wool Toupee

Bill Blaikie
Winnipeg-Transcontinental
NDP Shorn Sheep

Ethel Blondin-Andrew
Western Arctic
LIBERAL Musk Sheep

Morris Bodnar
Saskatoon Berry-Dundurn
LIBERAL Ram

Raymond Bonin
Nickel Belt-Roll of Quarters
LIBERAL Chops

Lucien Bouchard
Lac-Saint-Jean
BLOC Chevrier

Don Boudria
Glengarry-Prescott-Russell Baker
LIBERAL Shepherd

Cliff Breitkreuz
Yellowhead
REFORM Baaaaaa

Garry Breitkreuz
Yorkton-Melville-Herman
REFORM Baaaaaa

Margaret Bridgman
Surrey-Radical Fringe-North
REFORM Ewe

Pierre Brien
Témiscamingue
BLOC Mouton

Bonnie Brown
Oakville-Milton-John
LIBERAL No Spring Lamb

Jan Brown
Calgary Southeast Centre North
REFORM Goat

Dianne Brushett
Cumberland Gap-Coldturkey
LIBERAL Sheep

John Bryden
Hamilton-Wentworth
LIBERAL Ram

Charles Caccia
Davenport
LIBERAL Mutton

Murray Calder
Wellington-Grey-Dufferin-Simcoe-Valpy
LIBERAL Sheep

Barry Campbell
St. Paul's-Cathedral
LIBERAL Yarn

John Cannis
Scarborough Town Centre
LIBERAL Baaaaaa

René Canuel
Matapédia-Matane
BLOC Mouton

André Caron
Jonquière
BLOC Mouton

Marlene Catterall
Ottawa West Centre North
LIBERAL Lamb

PARLIAMENT HILL

Martin Cauchon
Outremont
LIBERAL Ram

Brenda Chamberlain
Guelph-Wellington
LIBERAL Ewe

Raymond Chan
Richmond-Virginia
LIBERAL Sheep

Jean Charest
Sherbrooke
PC Shorn Goat in Fleeced
Sheep's Clothing

David Chatters
Athabaska
REFORM Sheep

Jean Chrétien
Saint-Maurice-Chevalier
LIBERAL Goatherd
in Sheep's Clothing

Jean-Guy Chrétien
Frontenac
BLOC Mouton

Mary Clancy
Halifax
LIBERAL Mountain Goat

Shaughnessy Cohen
Windsor-St. Clair-de-Lune
LIBERAL Baaaaaa

David Collenette
Don Valley East North Centre
LIBERAL Night on Bald
Mountain Goat

Bernie Collins
Whiskey Sours-Moosehead
Beer Mountain
LIBERAL Mutton

Joe Comuzzi
Thunder Bay-Nipigon
LIBERAL Sheep

Sheila Copps
Hamilton East
LIBERAL Kid

Marlene Cowling
Dauphin-Swanee River
LIBERAL Chops

Rex Crawford
Norma Kent
LIBERAL Mutton

Paul Crête
Kamouraska-Rivière-du-Loup
BLOC Mouton

Harold Culbert
Carleton-Charlotte Gray
LIBERAL Sheep

John Cummins
Delta-Burke
REFORM Sheep in Goat's Clothing

Madeleine D. Dalphond-Guiral
Laval Centre
BLOC Mouton

Michel Daviault
Ahuntsic
BLOC Mouton

Simon de Jong
Regina-Je m'appelle
NDP Sheep in Shorn Sheep's Clothing

Pierre De Savoye
Portneuf-Complaint
BLOC Mouton

Bernard Deshaies
Abitibi
BLOC Mouton

Paul DeVillers
East Simcoe North
LIBERAL Mutton

Herb Dhaliwal
Vancouver Southwest Centre
LIBERAL Sheep in Goat's Clothing

David Dingwall
Cape Breton-East Richmond
LIBERAL Pork Barrel
in Goat's Clothing

Nick Discepola
Vaudreuil
LIBERAL Baaaaaa

Stan Dromisky
Thunder Bay-Atikokan
LIBERAL Ram

Antoine Dubé
Beavis-Butthead
BLOC Mouton

Gilles Duceppe
Laurier-Sainte-Marie-Among-
the-Hurons
BLOC Chevreau

Ron Duhamel
St. Boniface
LIBERAL Sheep

Maurice Dumas
Argenteuil-Papineau
BLOC Mouton

John Duncan
North Island North-Powell River
REFORM Lamb

Michel Dupuy
Laval North Centre West
LIBERAL in Kid Gloves

Wayne Easter
Malpeque
LIBERAL Sheep

Art Eggleton
York Centre East South
LIBERAL Goat
in Accountant's Clothing

John English
Kitchener
LIBERAL Three Bags Full

Ken Epp
Elk Island
REFORM Sheep

Ronald Fewchuk
Selkirk-Red River Cereal
LIBERAL Lamb

Gilbert Fillion
Chicoutimi
BLOC Mouton

Sheila Finestone
Mont Facelle Royale
LIBERAL No Spring Lamb

John Finlay
Oxford
LIBERAL Loin

Jesse Flis
Parkdale-High Park Duck Pond
LIBERAL Rack

Joe Fontana
London East
LIBERAL Sheep in Pencil-Thin
Moustache

Paul Forseth
New Westminister-Burnbaby Burn
REFORM Sheep

Jack Frazer
Club Saanich-Gulf Islands
REFORM Ram

Hedy Fry
Vancouver Centre Quadra East
LIBERAL Sheep in Goat's Clothing

Beryl Gaffney
Nepean
LIBERAL Mutton

Alfonso Gagliano
Saint-Léonard Cohen
LIBERAL Mountain Goat

Christiane Gagnon
Québec
BLOC Agneau du Printemps

Patrick Gagnon
Bonaventure-Îsles-de-la-Madeleine
LIBERAL Lamb

Roger Gallaway
Sarnia-Lambton's Naval Rum
LIBERAL Wooly Booly

Michel Gauthier
Roberval
BLOC Chèvre

Jon Gerrard
Portage-Interlake
LIBERAL Little Lost Lamb

Bill Gilmour
Comox-Alberni
REFORM Sheep

John Godfrey
Don Valley Centre West
LIBERAL Goat

Maurice Godin
Châteauguay
BLOC Mouton

Ralph Goodale
Regina Dentata-Wascana
LIBERAL Goat

Jim Gouk
Hootenanny West-Bevelspoke
REFORM Sheep

Bill Graham
Rosedale
LIBERAL Parchment

Herb Gray
Windsor West
LIBERAL Goat in Sheep's Clothing

Deborah Grey
Beaver Fever
REFORM Mountain Goat

Ivan Grose
Oshawa-Osh-Kosh-By-Gosh
LIBERAL Sheep

Herbert Grubel
Capillary-Howe-Now
REFORM Goat

Albina Guarnieri
Mississauga-Massassauga West East
LIBERAL Ewe

Monique Guay
Laurentides
BLOC Agneau du Printemps

Michel Guimond
Beauport-Montmorency-Orléans
BLOC Mouton

Art Hanger
Calgary Northeast Centre
REFORM Goat

Hugh Hanrahan
West Edmonton Mall-Strathcona Horse
REFORM Sheep

Mac Harb
Ottawa Civic Centre
LIBERAL Sheep

Edward Harper
Simcoe North Centre West
REFORM Goat

Elijah Harper
Churchill
LIBERAL Lamb

Stephen Harper
Calgary West Centre North
REFORM Divideth the hoof, but chews not the cud

Dick Harris
Prince George-Bulkley Valley
REFORM Ram

Jim Hart
Okanagan-Similkameen-Skinamarinky-Do
REFORM Sheep

John Harvard
Winnipeg-St. James Club
LIBERAL Baaaaaa

Sharon Hayes
Port Moody-PMS-Coquitlam
REFORM Three Bags Full

Elwin Hermanson
Kindersley-Lloydminster
REFORM Sheep in Goat's Clothing

Bonnie Hickey
St. John's East Centre West
LIBERAL Lamb

Grant Hill
Macleod
REFORM Lambaste

Jay Hill
Prince George-Paul-Ringo-Peace River
REFORM Sheep in Kid's Clothing

Jake Hoeppner
Lisgar-Marquette
REFORM Baaaaaa

Len Hopkins
Renfrew-Nipissing-Russell-Pembroke
LIBERAL Mutton

Charles Hubbard
Miramichi
LIBERAL Chops

Tony Ianno
Trinity-Spadina
LIBERAL Lamb

David Iftody
Provencher
LIBERAL Sheep

Ronald Irwin
Sault Ste. Marie
LIBERAL Salted Goat

Ovid Jackson
Bruce-Grey Generator
LIBERAL Ram

Jean-Marc Jacob
Charlesbourg
BLOC Chèvre

Daphne Jennings
Mission Furniture-Coquitlam
REFORM Sheep

Dale Johnston
Wetaskiwin
REFORM Ram

Jim Jordan
Leeds-Grenville
LIBERAL Mutton

Jim Karygiannis
Scarborough Town Centre-Agincourt
LIBERAL Sheep

Allan Kerpan
Moose Jaw-Lake Centre
REFORM Baaaaaa

Stan Keyes
North Hamilton West
LIBERAL Yarn

Bob Kilger
Stormont-Dundas
LIBERAL Wooly Booly

David Kilgour
West Edmonton Mall Southeast
LIBERAL Black Sheep

Gordon Kirkby
Prince Albert-Churchill River
LIBERAL Lamb

Gar Knutson
Elgin-Folktale
LIBERAL Sheep

Karen Kraft Sloan
York Centre-Simcoe
LIBERAL Ewe

Francine Lalonde
Mercier
BLOC Mouton

Jean Landry
Lotbinière
BLOC Mouton

François Langlois
Bellechasse
BLOC Mouton

Walter Lastewka
St. Catharines
LIBERAL Mutton

René Laurin
Joliette
BLOC Mouton

Laurent Lavigne
Beauharnois-Salaberry
BLOC Mouton

Raymond Lavigne
Verdun-Saint-Paul
BLOC Mouton

Ghislain Lebel
Chambly
BLOC Mouton

Francis LeBlanc
Cape Breton Highlands-Casino
LIBERAL Baaaaaa

Nic Leblanc
Longueuil
BLOC Mouton

Derek Lee
Scarborough-Rouge River
LIBERAL Sheep

Réjean Lefebvre
Champlain-Charlie
BLOC Mouton

Gaston Leroux
Richmond-Wolfe-Montcalm
BLOC Mouton

Jean Leroux
Shefford
BLOC Mouton

Clifford Lincoln
Lachine-Lac-St-Louis Laberge
LIBERAL Sheep in Goat's Clothing in Sheep's Clothing

John Loney
Edmonton Mall West North
LIBERAL Mutton

Yvan Loubier
Saint-Hyacinthe-Bagot
BLOC Mouton

Lawrence MacAulay
Cardigan-Sweater
LIBERAL Sheep in Kid's Clothing

Ronald MacDonald
Dartmouth
LIBERAL Lamb

Roy MacLaren
Etobicoke North Centre
LIBERAL Parchment

Russell MacLellan
Cape Breton-The Sydneys
LIBERAL Ram

Shirley Maheu
Saint-Laurent-Cartierville
LIBERAL Mutton

Gurbax Malhi
Bramalea-Gore-Malton
LIBERAL Sheep

John Maloney
Erie
LIBERAL Rack

John Manley
Ottawa Civic Centre South
LIBERAL Sheep in Sheep's Clothing

Preston Manning
Calvary-Southeast Centre North
REFORM Two horns like a lamb, and he spake as a dragon

Jean-Paul Marchand
Québec-Est
BLOC Mouton

Sergio Marchi
York Centre West
LIBERAL Ham in Goat's Clothing

Diane Marleau
Sudbury-Saturday Night
LIBERAL Lambikins

Keith Martin
Esquimalt-Juan de Fuchsia
REFORM Lamb

Paul Martin
LaSalle-Émard
LIBERAL Goat in Lambskin Gloves

Marcel Massé
Hull-Aylmer Canned Tomatoes
LIBERAL Parchment

Philip Mayfield
Cariboo-Chilcotin-Caboose
REFORM Baaaaaa

Ian McClelland
Edmonton Mall Southwest
REFORM Sheep

Larry McCormick
Hastings-Frontenac-Lennox-Annie
LIBERAL Mutton

Joe McGuire
Egmont
LIBERAL Sheep

Glen McKinnon
Brandon-Whiskey Souris
LIBERAL Lamb

Audrey McLaughlin
Yuk-Yuk's
NDP Shorn Sheep in Scapegoat's Clothing

Anne McLellan
Edmonton North West Mall
LIBERAL Sheep Wrapped in Parchment

Dan McTeague
Ontario
LIBERAL Sheep in Kid's Clothing

Edward McWhinney
Vancouver Quadraphenia Centre
LIBERAL Sheep

Réal Ménard
Hochelaga-Maisonneuve
BLOC Brebis

Paul Mercier
Blainville-Deux-Montagnes
BLOC Mouton

Val Meredith
Surrey-White Rock-S. Langley
REFORM Sheep in Kid's Clothing

Fred Mifflin
Bonavista-Trinity-Contraconception
LIBERAL Mutton

Peter Milliken
Kingston and the Islands
LIBERAL Sheep in Goat's Clothing

Bob Mills
Red Deer Cull
REFORM Baaaaaa

Dennis Mills
Broadview-Greenwood
Racetrack
LIBERAL Scapegoat

Maria Minna
Beaches-Woodbine Racetrack
LIBERAL Ewe

Andrew Mitchell
Parry Sound-Muskoka
LIBERAL Lamb

Lee Morrison
Swift Current-Maple Creek-Assiniboia
REFORM Mutton

John Murphy
Annapolis Valley-Hants
LIBERAL Sheep

Ian Murray
Lanark-Carleton
LIBERAL Ram

Bob Nault
Kenora-Rainy River
LIBERAL Lamb

Osvaldo Nunez
Bou-Bou-Bourassa
BLOC Mouton

John Nunziata
York South Centre-Weston
LIBERAL Black Sheep in Scapegoat's Clothing

Patrick O'Brien
London-Middlesex
LIBERAL Ram

John O'Reilly
Victoria-Chandler-Haliburton
LIBERAL Baaaaaa

André Ouellet
Papineau-Sainte-Michel
LIBERAL Chevrier

Rey Pagtakhan
Winnipeg North Centre South
LIBERAL Loin

Denis Paradis
Brome-Shopping Network-Missisquoi
LIBERAL Lamb

Philippe Paré
Louis-Hébert
BLOC Mouton

Gilbert Parent
Welland-St. Catharines-Stranglehold
LIBERAL Black Sheep

Carolyn Parrish
Mississauga Square One Centre West
LIBERAL Lamb

Bernard Patry
Pierrefonds-Dullard
LIBERAL Chops

Jean Payne
St. John's West Northeast
LIBERAL Mutton

Charlie Penson
Peace River
REFORM Baaaaaa

Janko Peric
Cambridge
LIBERAL Sheep

Doug Peters
Scarborough Town Centre East
LIBERAL Sheep in Kid's Clothing

Jim Peterson
Willowdale
LIBERAL Goat in Sheep's Clothing

Beth Phinney
Hamilton Molehill
LIBERAL Ewe

Pauline Picard
Drummond
BLOC Mouton

Jerry Pickard
Essex-Peter Kent
LIBERAL Sheep

Gary Pillitteri
Niagara Falls-Wine Barrel
LIBERAL Lamb

Louis Plamondon
Cardinal-Richelieu
BLOC Mouton

Roger Pomerleau
Anjou-Rivière-des-Prairies
BLOC Mouton

George Proud
Hillsborough
LIBERAL Mutton

Jack Ramsay
Crowfeet-Try Cucumbers
REFORM Black Sheep in Goat's Clothing

Julian Reed
David Halton-Emma Peel
LIBERAL Sheep

Geoffrey Regan
Halifax West Centre
LIBERAL Lamb

John Richardson
Perth-Wellington-Waterloo
LIBERAL Ram

George Rideout
Moncton
LIBERAL Baaaaaa

Nelson Riis
Kamloops de Loop
NDP Shorn Sheep in Kid's Clothing

Robert Ringma
Nanaimo Bar-Cowichan Sweater
REFORM Goat

Pierrette Ringuette-Maltais
Madawaska-Victoria
LIBERAL Lamb

Fernand Robichaud
Beauséjour
LIBERAL Lamb in Sheep's Clothing

Lucienne Robillard
St-Henri-Westmount
LIBERAL Goat in Parchment

Svend Robinson
Burnbaby Burn-Kingsway
NDP Goat in Kid's Clothing

Yves Rocheleau
Trois-Rivières
BLOC Mouton

Allan Rock
Etobicoke Centre North Centre
LIBERAL Goat

William Rompkey
Labrador-Retriever
LIBERAL Billy Goat in Sheep's Clothing

Benoît Sauvageau
Terrebonne
BLOC Mouton

Werner Schmidt
Okanagan Centre East
REFORM Baaaaaa

Andy Scott
Fredericton-York-Sunbury
LIBERAL Sheep

Mike Scott
Skeena-Dipping
REFORM Lamb

Benoît Serré
Timiskaming-French Dressing
LIBERAL Sheep

Alex Shepherd
Durham and Cheese
LIBERAL Ram

Georgette Sheridan
Saskatoon Berry-Humboldt
LIBERAL Ewe

Jim Silye
Calgary Centre Southeast
REFORM Scapegoat

Roger Simmons
Burin-St. George's
LIBERAL Sheep

Roseanne Skoke
Central Novacaine
LIBERAL Kid in Lamb
of God's Clothing

Monte Solberg
Medicine Cabinet
REFORM Kid

John Solomon
Regina Dentata-Lumsden
NDP Shorn Sheep

Ray Speaker
Lethbridge
REFORM Goat in Mountain
Sheep's Clothing

Bob Speller
Haldimand-Norfolk
LIBERAL Sheep
in Scapegoat's Clothing

Bernard St-Laurent
Manicouagan
BLOC Mouton

Brent St. Denis
Algoma
LIBERAL Mutton

Paul Steckle
Huron-Bruce Lee
LIBERAL Sheep in
Scapegoat's Clothing

Christine Stewart
Northumberland
LIBERAL Lamb in Kid's Clothing

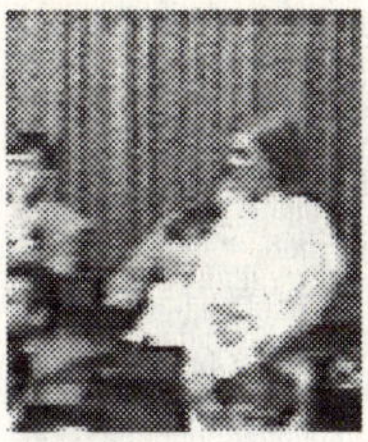

Jane Stewart
Brant
LIBERAL Lamb in Kid's Clothing

Darrel Stinson
Okanagan-Shuswap-Shuswap
REFORM Sheep

Chuck Strahl
Fraser Valley Centre East
REFORM Baaaaaa

Paul Szabo
Mississauga-Square
One-South Centre
LIBERAL Lamb

Len Taylor
The Battlefords-Meadow Lake
NDP Shorn Sheep

Andrew Telegdi
Waterloo-100 Days
LIBERAL Mutton

Anna Terrana
Vancouver Centre-
Quadraphenia East
LIBERAL Ewe

Peter Thalheimer
Timmins-Chapleau
LIBERAL Sheep

Myron Thompson
Wild Rose of Taxes
REFORM Billy Goat

Brian Tobin
Humber-St. Barbe-Baie Verte
LIBERAL Ham in Goat's Clothing

Paddy Torsney
Burlington
LIBERAL Lamb

Benoît Tremblay
Rosemont
BLOC Mouton

Suzanne Tremblay
Rimouski-Témiscouata
BLOC Mountain Goat

Rose-Marie Ur
Lambton-Middlesex-Babylon
LIBERAL Ewe

Tony Valeri
Lincoln-Alexander-Towncar
LIBERAL Ram

Lyle Vanclief
Prince Edward-Hasty-Pudding
LIBERAL Sheep

Pierrette Venne
Saint-Hubert-Chalet-Swiss
BLOC Agneau

Harry Verran
South West Nova Centre
LIBERAL Mutton

Joe Volpe
Eglinton-Lawrence
LIBERAL Baaaaaa

David Walker
East Winnipeg North Centre
LIBERAL Sheep

Tom Wappel
Scarborough Town Centre
North West
LIBERAL Scapegoat

Elsie Wayne
Saint John Tory
PC Fleeced Sheep

Derek Wells
South Shore
LIBERAL Mutton

Susan Whelan
Essex-Windsor Salt
LIBERAL Lamb

Randy White
Fraser Valley West
REFORM Sheep

Ted White
North Vancouver Quadraphenia
Centre
REFORM Sheep

John Williams
St. Albert Finney
REFORM Baaaaaa

Bob Wood
Nipissing Russell
LIBERAL Mutton

Douglas Young
Acadie-Bathurst Streetcar
LIBERAL Sheep

Paul Zed
Fundy-Royal
LIBERAL Sheep in Kid's Clothing

Commons Debates

April 18, 1996 1023997

Oral Questions

FURNITURE

Mr. Gilles Duceppe (Laurier-Sainte-Marie-Among-the-Hurons): Mr. Speaker, my quest…

Mr. Ray Speaker (Lethbridge): Yes, go ahead.

Mr. Speaker: I think he was addressing the chair.

Mr. Gilles Duceppe (Laurier-Sainte-Marie-Among-the-Hurons): Yes, actually, I thought I…

Mr. Ray Speaker (Lethbridge): Well, the chair can't answer him back. However, I can, so let him address me, not my damn chair.

Mr. Gilles Duceppe (Laurier-Sainte-Marie-Among-the-Hurons): Mr. Speaker, Mr. Speaker has obviously forgotten that the chair is also to be addressed as Mr.…

Mr. Ray Speaker (Lethbridge): Enough about the friggin' chair. Go ahead and talk to the damn furniture until you're blue in the face. Just don't drag me into it then.

Mr. Speaker: The member for Laurier-Sainte-Marie-Among-the Hurons will ask his question.

Mr. Gilles Duceppe (Laurier-Sainte-Marie-Among-the-Hurons): Mr. Speaker…

Mr. Ray Speaker (Lethbridge): Hello!

Some hon. members: Shurely shome mishtake.

Mr. Gilles Duceppe (Laurier-Sainte-Marie-Among-the-Hurons): …my question is for the Prime Minister. Given the long-standing embarrassment and mental suffering endured by Quebecers, will he dump the Hon. Michel Dupuy from Cabinet?

Right Hon. Jean Chrétien: I t'ank da hon. member for da 'istory lesson, but my hanswer is clear when I say as I 'ave so many time dat I yam proud to be a Canadian.

✖ ✖ ✖

EDUCATION

Herr Doktor Herbert Grubel (Capillary-Howe-Now): Mr. Speaker, I vas vonderink, vhat vas dis Reich – er, Goffernment – doink about ubereducation und underemployment amonk International Trade critic vhich vent to Yale?

Hon. Roy MacLaren (Minister of International Travel): Mr. Speaker, when I was in Harvard…

Mr. John Harvard (Winnipeg-St. James Club): Oooh, Oooh, Mr. Speaker, an important question of privilege!

Mr. Speaker: The hon. member on a question of privilege.

Mr. John Harvard (Winnipeg-St. James Club): I have hardly spoken with the minister more than a few times socially, and yet he now announces a disgusting intimacy with me which has never, ever, happened. Will the minister offer an immediate apology?

Roseanne Skoke (Central Novacaine): Shame, shame.

Hon. Roy MacLaren (Minister of International Travel): Mr. Speaker, I think…

Mr. Speaker: For crying out loud, can't a guy get any sleep around here? Yes! What is it now?

Hon. Roy MacLaren (Minister of International Travel): …the records clearly show I was in Harvard attending to graduate studies in business administration. I will gladly show the hon. member my degree if he wishes. Maybe I should have said "at Harvard" rather than "in." Will that help clear up this matter?

Mr. John Harvard (Winnipeg-St. James Club): All clear, Mr. Speaker.

Mr. Ray Speaker (Lethbridge): All clear? I don't even remember hearing the air-raid siren.

Most hon. members: Not you, pinhead!

Some hon. members: Lame, lame!

✖ ✖ ✖

GROAT

Hon. Jim Gouk (Hootenanny West-Bevelspoke): My question, Mr. Speaker…

Hon. Freestone Manna (Calvary-Southeast Centre North): Ray, don't even think about it!

Hon. Jim Gouk (Hootenanny West-Bevelspoke):…is for the Prime Minister. Can he explain just what this magical thing is that he calls "groat," and whether it can be raised by my constituents, who are looking for a replacement crop for canola?

Right Hon. Jean Chrétien (Prime Minister): Mr. Speaker, da member can fine dis kine of t'ing almost heverywhere da Liberals may be found to be da government. We 'ave stimulate da groat in da hinfrastructure, in da jobs, in da confidence of hall Canadian, an', hagainst great hodds, in da poll, of which I once hagain come out on da top dis month.

Hon. Jim Gouk (Hootenanny West-Bevelspoke): Mr. Speaker, my supplemental concerns this "hodds" the Prime Minister spoke of. Is that like a special fertilizer or something for groats? Can he table more information on all this?

Right Hon. Jean Chrétien (Prime Minister): Mr. Speaker, da 'onorable member is hobviously confuse. Hodds are like 25 to 1, not 20-20-20, or whatever it say on da bag of stuff you find in da Canadian Tire. It is no secret of dis government.

✖ ✖ ✖

PROCEEDS OF CRIME

[*translation*]

Hon. Lucien Bouchard (Leader of the Opposition): Mr. Speaker, struggling with the demons of depression over the recent severing of Quebec's one true chance at happiness and my chance to be president of something, I find myself truly a man without a country, without a home, without a purpose. I just want to be sure I am not a man without a pension too. Will I still get what is owing me?

Hon. Lucienne Robillard (Minister of Labour): Mr. Speaker, any answer to that is entirely hypothetical and is highly dependent upon the likelihood of the Leader of the Opposition meeting up in a dark alley with former prime minister Brian Mulroney.

✖ ✖ ✖

[*form of English*]

ETERNAL DAMNATION

Hon. Freestone Manna (Calvary-Southeast Centre North): Mr. Speaker, given the abysmally unresponsive posture this government has taken *vis-à-vis* the grass roots of this country, and their frustration in getting this government to live up to their promises, will this Prime Minister listen to my ringing indictment as put forth in the form of a pointless run-on question, or will he pretend not to hear the voice of all Canadians united and harmonizing with my own forthright cry for change, and resign immediately in my and my party's favour?

Right Hon. Jean Chrétien (Prime Minister): Er, no.

✖ ✖ ✖

JUST ICE

Hon. Myron Thompson (Wild Rose of Taxes): Mr. Speaker, my call for answerability and a full accounting is for the Minister of Gun Registration and Same-Sex Benefits. The other day when he bought some of us honourable committee members a round, was it neat, with a beer or water chaser, or what? My accountant wants to know.

Hon. Allan Rock (Etobicoke Centre North Centre): Just ice. I think, Mr. Speaker, what the member is groping for is Just Ice.

✖ ✖ ✖

HELL FREEZES OVER

Hon. Jean Charest (The Leader of Nothing): Me? Mr. Speaker, you're pointing to me? Are you sure? O.K. Is this thing on? Testing. One two three four. Actually I guess it should only be "One two," right, Elsie? Heh, heh! Anyways, as I was saying, I'm happy to be here in yet another church basement (*cont. p. 266*)

Questions orales. Oral questions. L'honorable chef de l'Opposition.

Thank you, Mr. Speaker. I am outraged that this government would insult Quebecers with money.

When will the Prime Minister understand we don't want your money? We just want to use your currency.

Mr. Speaker, what dat I yam 'ear from hover dere? Don't tell me. Next 'e tell me 'e don't want our foreign policy, jus' hour passport.

The Honourable Leader of the Opposition.

Thank you, Mr. Speaker. When will this Prime Minister understand Quebecers don't want your foreign policy, just your passports?

'Allo Mr. Speaker. Do you 'ear a hecho in dis place of question today? Maybe we should get t'ing fix.

The Honourable Member for Calgary Southwest.

Mr. Speaker, I am disgusted by this morbid dangling of the nation's future.

If the Prime Minister wants to dangle something, why not criminals from a rope? I swear on this stack of bibles, I would.

Dat is very interesting, Mr. Speaker. So what does dat 'ave to do wit' anyt'ing hanyone want to talk habout right now?

The Honourable Member for Calgary Something-or-other.

Mr. Speaker, that kind of dismissive attitude to the wishes of Canadians has put this government where it is. Er, governing.

Mr. Speaker, what can I say dat da leader of the oppos...ah da t'ird party...'as not for me made so clear. T'ank you. T'ank you.

The Honourable Member for Eskimo-Whatever.

Mr. Speaker, the Minister of Indian Affairs has the blood of everyone that ever bought a pack of smokes on his hands. What's he gonna do about it?

Pow! Take that, sucker. Pow! Pow! And that. Pow! Pow! Pow! Click. Click. Mr. Speaker, I'm out of ammo. Cover me.

Zzzzz...zzzzzzzzzz...zzzzzzzz...

Mr. Speaker, as a Reform Posse member, I found that almost funny. But not as funny as that frightful old thing in the bow tie.

Mr. Speaker, tell that cow-fancier that this fine suit has been to more top-class boat races than he's had hot bull testicles.

The Honourable Member for Yukon.

Mr. Speaker, I would like to ask the Minister of Human Resources, what is he doing?

Mr. Speaker, truthfully I find myself asking that more and more.

That's it, folks. Time's up. Go away. Or better yet, I'll go away. Kilgour! Get your butt out here and take over supervising these clowns.

Privy Council

The Privy Council is a conceit. Consisting of all ex–federal ministers, prime ministers, and former sports heroes, it never convenes as a body, except informally at key funerals and sporting events. Constitutionally, the Queen governs the country through the Governor General on the advice of the Privy Council or the Governor-in-Council, or the committee of the Privy Council, which are merely fancy, interchangeable names for the ministry or cabinet of the party in power. Other Privy Councillors, who hold the rank for life, cool their heels around the country waiting for the next big funeral or sporting event.

Privy Council

The Privy Council Office (PCO), however, truly exists, and is the hypothalamus of government. It serves as the secretariat to the Cabinet, and functions as the Prime Minister's government department or portfolio. Feared around Ottawa as the centre of bureaucratic power, it is housed in the Langevin Block, right by the Prime Minister's Office (PMO, see following), and spills out into a few other nearby buildings. While most of the politically sensitive operations of governing Canada are performed by the PMO, the PCO translates the emerging desires and wishes of Cabinet and the Prime Minister into bureaucratic action. The PCO also gathers and sifts and distributes the information needed by Cabinet to make even more decisions.

The Prime Minister has overall responsibility for the Privy Council and all its splendid, splintered glory. Chrétien shares some of this responsibility with Marcel Massé, the former bureaucrat, who is President of the Queen's Privy Council for Canada and Minister of Intergovernmental Affairs and Minister responsible for Public Service Renewal. Massé's section of the PCO is located over at 155 Queen Street, in a building whose floors and high-ceiling elevators thunder with the intense quiet of high mandarins. Reaching up to this level of elected power on behalf of the Public Service of Canada is the Clerk of the Privy Council. The current Clerk – Jocelyne Bourgon – serves as the head of the public service, the Prime Minister's Deputy Minister, and as the Secretary to the Cabinet. She is supposed to keep the public service functioning effectively, and advises Cabinet in a manner that keeps the decision-making process operating without disturbing either the system designed by the Prime Minister or his golf game.

During the Tory regime, the Clerk of the Privy Council became increasingly politicized, much to the pain of many civil servants. The PCO itself lost much of its policy-shaping influence to the PMO and outside advisors, and was reduced mainly to controlling the paper flow for Cabinet. Under Chrétien, things have slowly returned to traditional Liberal ways.

Jocelyne Bourgon, the first woman to serve as Clerk, has structured her PCO with about half a dozen top-tier civil servants:

deputy ministers, assistant deputy ministers, deputy clerks, or deputy secretaries who oversee a handful of secretariats, each with 5 to 20 officers, in turn overseen by an assistant secretary. From some of these secretariats ebb and flow the tides of paperwork for Cabinet committees. Agendas, memoranda to Cabinet/Discussion Papers, minutes of meetings, Committee Reports, and Records of Decisions, all move steadily and secretly. Other secretariats keep the wheels of government turning, or provide special support for the Prime Minister, such as the old Federal–Provincial Relations Office, for many years a semi-autonomous part of the PCO, now scrubbed of its Mulroney taint with the new moniker "Intergovernmental Affairs."

Privy Councillors, who hold the rank for life, cool their heels around the country waiting for the next big funeral or sporting event.

PCO staff are supposed to be the brightest members of the public service, and serve short tours of duty – of three to five years – before returning to other departments in their scramble for the mandarinate. Prized attributes are diplomacy, political sensitivity, helpful contacts across the civil service, and the ability to analyse problems and get their perspective out verbally or down neatly on paper before the timeliness of the analysis passes, or the minister loses interest.

The various secretariats used to support one of the many Cabinet committees that became fashionable during the Trudeau and Mulroney years. Under Chrétien there are only four Cabinet committees. Treasury Board has its own secretariat, and though the small Special Committee of Council looks intriguing and is chaired by the powerful Gray Herb, almost half of its few members are the weakest in the Cabinet – Marleau, Dupuy and Anderson. It performs more of an oversight or review role, and is best avoided. Policy is funnelled through either Economic Development or Social Development, which gives the PCO pointy heads more time to problem-solve now that they don't have to babysit a hectic Cabinet committee, agenda and schedule. Of course, that removes some of the fun and power of being a PCO deputy clerk or secretary, but such is the sacrifice for the public service.

One aspect of the PCO that is often overlooked is the increasing intelligence, or spook, role it plays. When the national-security mania that usually attends American administrations infected the Muldoon government, it caused swellings of budgets, staffs, and egos of the traditionally relaxed Canadian practitioners. A handful of secretariats and the Canadian Security Intelligence Review Committee, which oversee the Canadian Security Intelligence Service (CSIS), all channel the flow to the Prime Minister. And the PCO's traditional secrecy makes it nearly impossible to monitor for abuse or cock-ups, creating such an effective cloak that most Canadians and parliamentarians don't know about it.

Government of Canada / Gouvernement du Canada
Privy Council Office / Bureau du Conseil privé

HOUSE OF COMMONS BOOK - BRIEFING NOTE
LIVRE DE LA CHAMBRE DES COMMUNES - NOTES D'INFORMATION

Agency / Agence: Us.

Classification: Cross your heart & hope to die

Subject/Highlights / Sujet/Point salliants

Somehow the media has come to learn of Jacques Parizeau's homard comment to the Dutch Ambassador.

Source

Eddie.

Suggested Reply / Réponse suggérée

My, M. Parizeau seems to be buttering Quebecers up, doesn't he?

I always thought M. Parizeau preferred crow.

He would say that, wouldn't he?

The person responsible for this breach of security will be found and severely dealt with. This kind of flagrant disregard for international and national confidences chews at the very joists of our interdependent world which can only continue to...etc., etc.

Assessment / Évaluation

Somehow an internal memo reached the hands of La Presse (please send waybill onto Treasury Board for settlement). Publication should be very soon.

The memo by Michel Duval recounted private communications from the Dutch Ambassador, Jan Fietelaars, detailing the Premier of Quebec's horrible pomposity and bone-headed choice of words to describe his opinion of Quebecers after voting in favour of his referendum question.

Er, everything worked out just as we had discussed. Our point!

Prepared by / Prépare par	Division	Date	Approved by / Approvė par
Claude Morin	9 into 81is 9.	July 04.95	M. Massé

Prime Minister's Office

The Prime Minister's Office was originally embedded within the PCO, but was pulled out by Pierre Trudeau. It serves as a hypersensitive political nerve ganglion for the Prime Minister of the day, and is highly partisan. The PMO takes care of protocol and travel; manages the Prime Minister's schedule, access, and tee-times; prepares him for Question Period and other public appearances; handles the flood of correspondence; keeps him in contact with the party machinery; spins the media; winnows through the piles of patronage and Governor-in-Council appointees; helps set policy priorities, parliamentary strategy, electoral timing; and provides crisis management.

The Prime Minister has two physical offices – one in the Centre Block used for photo-ops and interviews, and the "real" office across Wellington Street, in the Langevin Block. With him in the Langevin Block are most of his support staff, presently about 69 strong (roughly the same numbers as in the last years of Tory rule). It is a diverse collection of talents and personalities, some sharing decades of history with Chrétien, others interchangeable, but all tenaciously and quietly loyal.

In a city always attuned to titles, the term "assistant" crops up in 38 of the 69 positions, with only 20 of those being plain, unencumbered "assistants." There are 7 Special Assistants; 5 Executive Assistants; 2 Research Assistants; 2 Correspondence Assistants; a Personnel Assistant; and an Assistant Manager.

Prime Minister's office Langevin Block

Like the Mulroney office, and most PMOs for the last 20 years, the ranking staff hails from Quebec. Lester B. Pearson once told Chrétien; "The biggest mistake we ever made in Canada was when Queen Victoria chose Ottawa over Montreal as the capital," though nobody told Montrealers. Or they didn't notice. Yet, where Muldoon took heat for continuing the dominance of "the Montreal Mafia" over the public life of this country, Chrétien hasn't. Muldoon's PMO might have gotten a new copper roof; Chrétien's metaphorically got a thick coat of Teflon.

Maintaining that Teflon begins each morning at 8:45, when the senior staff meets for a strategy session to try to co-ordinate that day's goal, and tease out spins for detected or anticipated problems. The Prime Minister's tee-time is also confirmed.

There are basically two firm principles behind Chrétien's PMO. The first is his belief that "the stronger and more intelligent the officials, the better the minister." And the other he picked up from Mitchell Sharp's observation: "The smaller the Office, the more powerful the occupant."

Rating the PMO according to the Mitchell Sharp Principle:

"The smaller the Office, the more powerful the occupant."

Personal Adviser to the Prime Minister	1	Operations	4
Sr. Policy Adviser	2	Finance, Personnel and Administration	5
Legislative Assistant	2	Prime Minister's Correspondence	7
Special Adviser – Caucus	2	Communications	10
Photographer	2	Regional Assistants	10
Chief of Staff	4	Policy and Research	11
Appointments	4		

CHRETIEN'S ADVISERS: Aline to Zussman

Aline Chrétien: Wife of the Prime Minister. Mrs. Chrétien hails, like her husband, from Shawinigan. They were married in 1957, with Jean starting his political career six years later. Constantly at his side, she is a quiet presence: seen and rarely heard. For instance, she gave no interviews during the 1993 campaign.

Aline Chrétien

There is no Parliament Hill office and staff for Aline – she does whatever work is required out of 24 Sussex. Jean publicly credits her with advising him to drop the TelePrompTer and stiff public image that hurt him after he won the 1990 leadership race. And he claims she provides intelligent counsel based on observing others while he's busy pressing the flesh and doing his folksy public shtick. In fact, most glimpses of her come through comments by Jean. Her low profile might seem part of the "if Mulroney did it, we won't" Chrétien strategy, but it has been quite consistent for over 30 years. Genuinely private, and intelligent enough to keep it that way.

Jocelyne Bourgon: Clerk of the Privy Counsel, PCO. Ms. Bourgon is Deputy Minister to the Prime Minister, the head of the Public Service, and Secretary to the Cabinet. She travels along a most challenging razor wire between partisanship and sober, professional detachment. While such predecessors during the Tory years as Paul Tellier and Glen Shortliffe snuggled up to the government, much to the disappointment of civil servants, the Liberals have quieter ways of naturally influencing the process. Long years of power created a tight fit between Grit and the PCO. Chrétien's Marcel Massé himself was a former Clerk, and the ways of Clerk Michael Pitfield still haunt the corridors of the PCO. In fact, Ms. Bourgon was well mentored by Gérard Veilleux during his mandarin days at Treasury Board and Federal–Provincial Relations, and before his unforeseen madness set in at the CBC.

Ms. Bourgon started out at Transport in 1974, and then collected the usual mix of departments that signal a hot public-service prospect: Fisheries and Oceans; Department of Regional and Industrial Expansion; Federal–Provincial Relations Office; and Energy, Mines and Resources. (It was at Fisheries that Veilleux found her and made her a "star.") By all accounts very capable and bright, she is also considered tough and yet diplomatic enough to hold intact the public service's remaining integrity and power. The Clerk is responsible for keeping Cabinet and its business orderly and functional, and gives advice to Chrétien on policy and key public-service appointments, which is then subject to riders, counter-advice, and neglect from the Prime Minister's crew at the PMO.

Given the leaner PMO, and the natural mind-meld between Liberals and senior public servants, it's natural that Chrétien has announced his ministry will rely much more on the PCO for policy than Muldoon did. While ranking members of the PCO may admire and identify with televison's Sir Humphrey Appleby, the Canadian halls of power are really *Yes, Minister* and *Yes, Prime Minister* without the jokes. Any jokes.

Penny Collenette: Director of Appointments, PMO. Mrs. Collenette has been a long-time Chrétien loyalist. Her service goes back through the 1984 and 1990 leadership bids. She also was part of the cadre of Chrétien loyalists hanging around with Eddie Goldenberg (see following) during the Turner wilderness years. She is now in charge of the extremely powerful and deadly force of government patronage. Or, as she likes to call it, "talent scouting." That means prospecting through the piles of party loyalists petitioning for jobs, and matching the worthy and the unworthy to appropriate positions the PCO has identified as being within the prerogative of the Prime Minister.

Along with her slap-headed front-bench husband, Defence Minister David Collenette, the pair's combined tag-team career weight makes them the top power couple in Canada. Sort of a Bob and Elizabeth Dole, only younger, nicer, and duller, on Prozac and Metamucil.

Jean Carle

Jean Carle: Operations Director, PMO. Sort of the young, quiet mystery man of the Chrétien circle. He joined Chrétien as Executive Assistant in 1990, when he served as gatekeeper of the OLO (Office of the Leader of the Opposition) by controlling access to Chrétien. For a while he even lived with the Chrétien family. Carle is given credit for the smooth running of the 1993 campaign, in which the media were swallowed up in physical and professional comfort, near-flawless scheduling, and constant attention.

He sweats the details in the PMO, arranging the schedule, travel, tee-times.

He said what?

I think we can take that to mean that what he really meant to say was, uh...
Peter Donolo

Peter Donolo: Communications Director, PMO. It is an amazing country when the former speech writer and media adviser to the most boring mayor in recent Canadian history – Art Eggleton – can become the chief spin doctor for the Prime Minister. But considering that Eggleton escaped without notice or taint from a stunning period of corruption in Toronto, that might not be a bad recommendation.

Donolo grew up in Mount Royal and went to Lower Canada College. He joined Chrétien in 1991, and is credited with helping to lessen media hostility, and (along with Aline) with freeing Chrétien from scripts and TelePrompTers. Chrétien's ActionMan stunts and the famous blue denim shirt were Donolo's calculated spins to fix problems. Yet Donolo, as director of communications and official spokesman during the 1993 campaign, began to irritate journalists with his constant, cheery wind-sniffing and fart-catching – though not enough to do any damage to the Prime Minister. He has also reamed out Liberal caucus members like Sheila Copps, in an effort to keep Chrétien awash in a pea-green sea of popularity, which doesn't do much for his own. However, he's still liked well enough to spin on.

I think we can take that to mean that what he really meant to say was, uh...
Eddie

Edward Goldenberg, a.k.a "Eddie," "Goldenschlong": Senior Policy Adviser, PMO. Tiny bachelor Eddie Goldenberg has been an object of persistent, yet ultimately unfulfilling, investigation and probing by the media and opponents for well over a decade. Not athletic, but said to easily fill an athletic supporter, Goldenberg manages to survive an annual canoe trip to the Canadian North with buddies like CTV's Craig Oliver and other political junkies.

Born of parents firmly established in the political backrooms of Montreal and the halls of McGill University, Eddie joined Chrétien at Treasury Board in 1975 after earning a McGill law degree. Over the intervening years, Eddie has been inseparable from Jean. He's been called Jean's security blanket, or Jiminy Cricket, and much worse. Some even suspect he tucks Chrétien in at night. He's gone with Jean on every stop of his ministerial career. And when the boss lost to Turner in 1984, Eddie later followed him to the new Ottawa branch of Toronto's Lang Michener Cranston Farqharson and Wright.

I yam not worry. Why should you be worry? For you hall to make someone like me so popular, I must 'ave something going for me.

Hall is well. And if not, den we make it so, as we halways do.

Ain't dat right, Eddie? Eddie?

Seem I lose my halter-hego. Anyone seen da brainy liddle guy?

Dere he go, with Peter, against great hodds to pull da plug on da camera and mike before I say what it is I should not be.

Hurry up dere, boys, I yam running out of folksy banality and dose funny little story.

What's more, Eddie assisted Jean as a key player in Trudeau's constitutional reforms, both becoming acknowledged experts in constitutional matters – an understanding that serves them well now.

During the Turner years, Eddie kept the Chrétien loyalist corps together, working the phones and using informal weekends at his cottage north of Ottawa. This gave Chrétien a running start when Turner resigned as leader. Yet, on the eve of Chrétien's succession to the leadership, Goldenberg, John Rae (see following), and Chrétien's constitutional advisor Eric Maldoff were discovered working behind the scenes in an attempt to salvage the Meech Lake Accord, though Jean was slyly offering up the appearance of being a Trudeau Liberal opposed to the deal. Strangely, this episode (with some memorable CBC footage of Goldenberg trying to flee a CBC crew that spotted him plotting with the Tories) didn't stick to Chrétien. And it just confirmed Eddie's legendary political opportunism.

Eddie served as principal secretary in Chrétien's Office of the Leader of the Opposition, but everyone admits his term was disastrous. Resolutely protective and loyal to Jean, Eddie pissed off members of the Liberal caucus and party who tried unsuccessfully to get to the leader, either directly or through Eddie. Even Jean admits in his autobiography that his office wasn't "functioning very well because I lacked a strong manager to run it properly" – but he never pointed directly at his old friend. Things began to turn around when Chrétien recruited Jean Pelletier to run the office as Chief of Staff, and Eddie stayed with what he does best: policy wonking and political fixing.

Because of his intensely shy, awkward, and private nature – dusted with a bit of disarming joviality – and the iron wall he maintains about his relationship to Chrétien, a lot of whispered resentment follows Eddie about. But the carps are mainly from enemies who have crossed swords with him in political battles. The least hostile and least toadying reviews of their working relationship say that Eddie has always provided Jean with unrelentingly concise and clear summations of problems and workable options or responses, allowing an undistracted politician to pick one, knowing it will be carried out exactly as presented.

Chaviva Hošek: Director of Policy and Research, PMO, and co-author of the Red Book. An enigma wrapped up inside a pita of chilling intelligence and dressed with personal political disappointment. She has an impeccable, feared reputation for brilliance that began during her graduate studies at Harvard. Since then she spent 13 years teaching English at the University of Toronto before rising to the top of the National Action Committee on the Status of Women. Her notoriety grew when she managed to bluff the leaders into a special televised debate on women's issues during the 1984 federal election. Next stop was Gordon Capital, where she functioned as some sort of consultant. Then the Ontario Liberals came calling and turned her into a star candidate in 1987. (Chrétien was also at Gordon Capital's Montreal office as some vague consultant after 1986.) As Minister of Housing for David Peterson, Ms. Hošek was flayed alive by the media and special interests, and was not helped by her demonstrating all the political *bonhomie* of a baking mud flat. The Patti Starr scandal helped suck her down, and she was dumped by Peterson, who has consistently demonstrated all the intelligence of a baking mud flat. Finally put out of her provincial misery in 1990, Ms. Hošek ended up working as a policy wonk, at Chrétien's invitation.

Her office on the first floor of the Langevin Building belonged to Imelda Muldoon. It amuses Chaviva and yet punishes her with the brutality of Mrs. Muldoon's design choices, since Chrétien has severely limited the traditional orgy of power office renovations. It could also point to her status since the Liberals have become safely tucked in government – the Red Book has about the same policy weight as a dated election poster (her co-creator Paul Martin has officially announced the financial portions long dead, screaming, "screw the Red Book!").

Michael McAdoo: Executive Assistant, PMO. A young oak growing amid a grove of ancient oaks. Or at least the latest Executive Assistant in a circle dominated by former EAs like Goldenberg, Carle, and the telephonically enhanced John Rae (see following). McAdoo has no little power in the PMO – he's one of those who control access to the Prime Minister.

Given Jean's talent for talent spotting, McAdoo's future in the Liberal party is assured, but his likelihood of reaching the status of his predecessors is piss-poor, unless Jean holds power well into the next century.

Jean Pelletier

Jean Pelletier: Chief of Staff, PMO. The defeated Liberal candidate for Quebec City in the last election, Pelletier was immediately offered the post of Chief of Staff in the Prime Minister's Office. Pelletier accepted, and runs the PMO with authority, stability, and managerial efficiency. An old college friend of Chrétien's at Trois-Rivières, Pelletier first served as Chief of Staff during Chrétien's difficult time as Leader of the Opposition, where he managed to bring order to an unruly caucus and a party machine that was grumbling at the aloofness of Eddie Goldenberg.

John Rae

White-haired and firm of manner, he adds a needed professional tone to Chrétien's machine, which otherwise would function too much like a family, right down to the petty fights, jealousies, resentments, and emotional scars. He has quietly spent the years since 1991 trying to fix Chrétien's image with the francophone press. To a degree, it has worked.

John Rae: Rapid Deployment Force, Power Corporation. The older brother of Norma Bob Rae, John was spotted by Chrétien as a potential spear-carrier and adviser when the Rae family was in Geneva back in 1966. One of those damned Queen's University Political Studies graduates, he joined Jean as his first assistant at Indian and Northern Affairs in 1967. Chrétien's been trying to hang on to him ever since. When Rae left Chrétien's office in 1971, it was to join Paul Desmarais's Power Corporation, something Jean helped arrange. And from Power Corp., Rae has continued to provide career-making assistance and money whenever he, and it, have been needed, managing or chairing the two leadership contests and the last election for Chrétien.

Mitchell Sharp: Personal Adviser to the Prime Minister, PMO. Brought in as a $1-a-year man in a gesture designed to evoke nostalgia for a long-dead era of Liberalism, Sharp really is the creator of Jean Chrétien – something Chrétien readily and repeatedly acknowledges in his autobiography, *Straight from the Heart*, with the tender scenes of their relationship and growth almost cinematically unspooling across the screen like those between Gepeto and Pinocchio.

Sharp, of course, is one of those types that gives Reform middle-benchers the willies, with his Trilateral Commission pedigree, Deputy Minister service, and London School of Economics education.

Though nearing 85, Sharp helped sift through Chrétien's Cabinet appointees for conflicts of interest and ethical cancers. He's long been interested in trying to restore admiration for the public service through ethical government. Yet, given his abhorrence of even the perception of questionable integrity, one would love to have heard his advice on any of Heritage Minister Michel Dupuy's escapades, or the Cabinet's helpful support of Power Corp.– controlled Power DirecTV. But perhaps, he wasn't asked. If he was, then the Liberals got as good as they paid for.

Hon. Mitchell Sharp

Howard Wilson: Ethics Counsellor, umbilical cord to the PMO. Not in the political loop. More like political window-dressing. Probably in the running for the loneliest public servant in Ottawa – the Maytag repairman of the bureaucratic world. And a likely candidate for the next "wrongful hiring" suit slapped by a civil servant on the government (see Public Service section).

Chrétien announced in 1994 that Mr. Wilson was someone "who will have teeth to investigate and take action." And sure enough, there was Howard in the press reports, grinning away, demonstrating the fact that, yes, he does have teeth. The office was originally to be at arm's length, back when the Red Book was taken seriously.

The Ethics Counsellor's Office, folded in with the Conflict of Interest Registry, is part of the great Liberal reform of the lobbying industry. So far neither Michel Dupuy's nor the Prime Minister's close ties to Power Corp. have unduly upset the office.

David Zussman: until recently Assistant Secretary, PCO. Considered by many to be the model of PCO geek breeding, with stints at External Affairs, Energy, Mines and Resources as well as the PCO, Zussman first left the public service in 1984 and spent the Mulroney years at Ottawa University as Dean of the Faculty of Administration and as president of Environics-DRZ Inc. Ironically, he became the bogeyman of thousands in the public service during Chrétien's first two years. Now he's returning again to the University of Ottawa, and intends to write a gripping wonk book.

Chrétien first utilized Zussman in 1982, lifting him from the PCO to make him senior policy adviser at Energy, Mines and Resources. Like other important advisers collected over the years, Zussman was coaxed back into service during the 1990 leadership race, and served Chrétien as a part-time policy adviser. He was readily acknowledged years ago as an important player if and when Chrétien took power. With the Liberal victory in 1993, Zussman was given the task of planning the transition to power and the internal structure of the new Liberal government. Though flagged as a contender for clerk of the Privy Council, Zussman was also said to be pissed about the damage done to the ranks of senior bureaucrats and the flushing of high-level women to lower ranks by Kim Campbell and ex-Clerk Glen Shortliffe just before the 1993 election. As a result, he probably had a hand in Chrétien's appointment of Jocelyne Bourgon as Clerk, while he settled in at the Programme Review/ Machinery of Government secretariat as Assistant Secretary. His task there has been to identify and remove unnecessary civil servants, using clues provided in an extensive review of all 22 government departments. How many thousands of jobs this may be has yet to be fully tallied, but the lists grow longer.

So far the first big Chrétien player to leap back into the "real world," where he'll continue to help out as needed.

While Chrétien has claimed there'll be no Kitchen Cabinet – non-government people who offer advice and undercut the official stream of advisers and policy fanatics – during his government, there are a couple of men whose phone calls sure as hell won't go unanswered:

Gérard Veilleux: President, Power Communications Inc. A slick ex-mandarin, a former Treasury Board secretary, and ineffectual, delusional former president of the CBC, Veilleux has had close ties to the PM since 1966, when Chrétien first needed help getting up to speed as Mitchell Sharp's parliamentary secretary. In 1980/81, the two worked closely during the endless constitutional negotiations and discussions. With Zussman, Veilleux helped set up the current Liberal paper-pushing structure in the PCO and Cabinet. He is also credited with "discovering" bureaucrat Jocelyne Bourgon, guiding her steadily through the top levels of the public service. In July 1994, he finished a useful report for the new Liberal Treasury Board that absolved the government from any sin that resulted from using the patronage system to staff 48 Crown corporations.

David Zussman

Playing somewhat fast and loose with government conflict lines, Veilleux slid into the Power Communications Inc. presidency, setting up a paper firewall to keep him from the extensive electronic broadcast side of the operation until his year-long ethical decompression period from the CBC ended in November 1994. He claims he now has more of a strategic-planning job, which makes perfect sense, given the great "success" of his repositioning exercise at CBC-TV. Along with John Rae and Chrétien's son-in-law, André Desmarais, Veilleux reminds one that Power Corporation is not misnamed.

Robert Nixon: Gentleman farmer. The former Ontario Treasurer has already done service for Chrétien in producing the quick report that led to the Liberal cancellation of the Pearson International Airport privatization agreement. With a circle of advisers so heavily gathered from Montreal, Nixon is a tiny voice of counsel from hated Ontario. Nixon is also father of one Jane (*née* Nixon) Stewart, the Liberal MP for Brant, an up-and-comer who does lots of media appearances.

Office of the Prime Minister

Cabinet du Premier ministre

The PMO Press Office

presents

The Right Honourable Jean Chrétien

in

The FOUR Seasons

Office of the
Prime Minister

Cabinet du
Premier ministre

Ottawa, Canada K1A 0A2

Notice

For Immediate Release

September 25, 1995

Prime Minister Jean Chrétien will play golf again today, have some dinner, and get a good night's sleep.

- 30 -

**PMO Press Office:
(613) 957-5555**

Avis

Diffusion immédiate

Le 25 septembre 1995

Le premier ministre Jean Chrétien a jouera le golf et goof off ce soir.

- 30 -

**Service de presse du CPM:
(613) 957-5555**

Office of the Prime Minister

Cabinet du Premier ministre

Ottawa, Canada K1A 0A2

Notice

Avis

For Immediate Release

December 11, 1995

Prime Minister Jean Chrétien will have a good night's sleep after dinner, which will follow a discussion of golf with Ontario Premier Mike Harris.

- 30 -

PMO Press Office:
(613) 957-5555

Diffusion immédiate

Le 11 décembre 1995

Après une discussion de golf avec le premier ministre d'Ontario Mike Harris, le premier ministre Jean Chrétien mangera un repas et se coucher.

- 30 -

Service de presse du CPM:
(613) 957-5555

Office of the Prime Minister | Cabinet du Premier ministre

Ottawa, Canada K1A 0A2

Notice

For Immediate Release

March 4, 1996

Prime Minister Jean Chrétien will play golf again today in Florida, have some dinner, and get a good night's sleep.

- 30 -

PMO Press Office:
(613) 957-5555

Avis

Diffusion immédiate

Le 4 mars 1996

Le premier ministre Jean Chrétien a joué le golf en Floride et wrestle three alligators avant de nager to Cuba pour la nuit. Âllo, est-ce-que personne lit ça?

- 30 -

Service de presse du CPM:
(613) 957-5555

Office of the
Prime Minister

Cabinet du
Premier ministre

Ottawa, Canada K1A 0A2

Notice

Avis

For Immediate Release

June 18, 1996

Prime Minister Jean Chrétien will have some dinner after playing golf, and get a good night's sleep.

- 30 -

PMO Press Office:
(613) 957-5555

Diffusion immédiate

Le 18 juin 1996

Le premier ministre Jean Chrétien va jouer le golf et ... Christ sur bicyclette c'est ennuyeux. Ça c'est de la merde. Je m'en fiche!

- 30 -

Service de presse du CPM:
(613) 957-5555

Cabinet

Cabinet is the functional bit of the Privy Council that operates as the Committee of the Privy Council. It is filled with semi-regular infusions of new or old Privy Councillors, selected by the Prime Minister from among sitting members of the House of Commons or the Senate. The Prime Minister settles on this Committee of the Privy Council, or his ministry, using a number of hoary old political chestnuts about regional, linguistic, and gender representation, all within the confines of political debts and talent pool.

The current Cabinet structure was determined by two political needs: to have fewer members at the big table than the previous government, and to set up a system of possible promotion to keep the hordes of newly elected Liberals disciplined and hopeful. Thus there are 23 full ministers ($46,645) around the Prime Minister ($69,920), with another 8 semi-ministers, or secretaries of state, pulling in about 3/4 of a minister's salary. Chrétien

Da polls show no crisis in federalism. Give it some time an' money. It will change back.

Everyt'ing change back to da way it was once. I've seen it hall hover da year.

As da singing Byrds say, "Turn, turn, turn."

Now wit' da separatists, it is dere turn to be hup. It was our turn, an' before it was hagain dere turn, an' so on.

We have a strategy for a united Canada. How many time do I 'ave to say so. Quebecer will not separate. 'ow do I know?

Because da singing Byrds don't honly tell. Eddie tell me.

has also windily expanded the importance of parliamentary secretaries ($10,500) serving each minister, who are not Privy Councillors but have been anointed by the Prime Minister as having Cabinet potential. So a small working Cabinet is spun out to another 31 positions.

Ministers quickly fade from our collective memory. One need only flip through old Peter C. Newman and Richard Gwyn books to realize how utterly foreign, forgettable, and obtuse former ministers and their trials look years later. One doesn't even need to go back that far. Glance over Erik Nielsen's *The House Is Not a Home*, and the same feelings rise up. So what? is the overwhelming response. And that is the greatest fear of all ministers while in office. Smart bureaucrats and lobbyists play gently on a minister's childish need to leave a lasting mark in order to get what they want. And it often works.

As for work, most ministers oversee a department or two, plus a handful of boards, tribunals, or agencies. They defend these from colleagues at the Cabinet table, from assaults in the House, and against the media and public. While Cabinet usually meets once a week, at 22 bodies it is too large for fidgety work. The agenda maintained by the Clerk of the Privy Council keeps the full Cabinet to limited discussion and saying yea or nay to the decisions needed to govern. The actual work of Cabinet is done by smaller Cabinet committees, to which problems, important information, proposed policies, and legislation are channelled through a system of memoranda and reports. The summaries, called Committee Reports, are placed on the full Cabinet agenda; if no disagreement is raised, the agenda is entered in the Record of Decision, which is sort of an official scrapbook of government policy as determined by Cabinet. Chrétien has hacked back the vast array of Cabinet committees he inherited to four: Treasury Board, which controls government expenditure; the Special Committee, which reviews proposed legislation; and two policy committees, Economic Development Policy and Social Development Policy. The Prime Minister will set up ad hoc committees to deal with unexpected issues, but they are temporary and limited.

Because some of the Committee Reports will split a Cabinet like a maul splintering dead wood, Cabinet fights and screaming matches are kept secret for 30 years, denying the opposition and media the chance to heckle losers and exploit differences. The maintenance of this kind of secrecy, literally papering over huge rifts, is the keystone of collective responsibility and Cabinet solidarity. If a Cabinet battle is leaked to the press (if it doesn't come from the PMO for management reasons), the repercussions on suspected ministers can be painful and embarrassing. Perk withdrawal can be a horrible thing to see.

Chrétien Cabinet Committees

Economic Development Policy

Chair
The Hon. André Ouellet

Vice-Chair
The Hon. Anne McLellan

Members
The Hon. Lloyd Axworthy
The Hon. David Collenette
The Hon. Roy MacLaren
The Hon. Ralph Goodale
The Hon. David Dingwall
The Hon. Brian Tobin
The Hon. Sheila Copps
The Hon. John Manley
The Hon. Douglas Young
The Hon. Marcel Massé
The Hon. Lucienne Robillard

Treasury Board

Chair
The Hon. Arthur Eggleton

Vice-Chair
The Hon. Paul Martin

Members
The Hon. David Anderson
The Hon. David Dingwall
The Hon. Sergio Marchi
The Hon. Marcel Massé

Social Development Policy

Chair
The Hon. Sheila Copps

Vice-Chair
The Hon. Marcel Massé

Members
The Hon. Herbert Gray, P.C.
The Hon. Lloyd Axworthy
The Hon. Ron Irwin
The Hon. Brian Tobin
The Hon. Joyce Fairbairn
The Hon Sergio Marchi
The Hon. Diane Marleau
The Hon. Michel Dupuy
The Hon. Allan Rock

Special Committee of Council

Chair
The Hon. Herbert Gray

Vice-Chair
The Hon. Allan Rock

Members
The Hon. David Anderson
The Hon. Diane Marleau
The Hon. Douglas Young
The Hon. Michel Dupuy
The Hon. Anne McLellan

The Canadian Ministry a.k.a. Cabinet Order of Precedence

THE RIGHT HON. JEAN CHRÉTIEN
PRIME MINISTER
Prime Minister's Office
Privy Council Office

- Canadian Centre for Management Development
- National Round Table on the Environment and the Economy
- Official Residences Council
- National Advisory Board for Science and Technology
- Canadian Security Intelligence Review Committee

THE HON. HERB GRAY, P.C.
Leader of the Government in the House of Commons and Solicitor General of Canada

Department of the Solicitor General

- Canadian Security Intelligence Service (CSIS)
- Correctional Service Canada (CSC)
- National Parole Board (NPB)
- Royal Canadian Mounted Police (RCMP)
- Office of Correctional Investigator
- Office of Inspector General
- RCMP External Review Committee
- RCMP Public Complaints Commission
- Office of Chief Electoral Officer

Gray Herb was first elected to the Commons in 1962, and is the longest-serving MP on the benches and in Cabinet. Born in Windsor, Herb escaped the fate of merely being Gurarie rather than Gray when Canadian immigration officials misspelled the Byelorussian surname of his parents. Radiating indiscernible charisma, at least until the arrival of Reform recalibrated the scale, Herb is chief political minister for Ontario. He is also de facto deputy prime minister, something that even Sheila Copps understands.

He has a fairly good handle on caucus, and can be depended on to crack his whips and backbenchers about if the somewhat overhyped Liberal backbench revolts continue to grow. Almost as aged and observant, and certainly the same colour as the gargoyles on the Peace Tower, Gray Herb knows where the skeletons rattle, and has the veteran wiles to know how to snare the bumper crop of rookies who haven't yet accumulated dry bones. Another in the unending procession of lawyer-politicians, Herb pledged to shepherd through a parliamentary reform package promised in the Red Book, loosening the party discipline on votes, but that has yet to happen. Some attempts at reforming MPs' pensions have started, to no great acclaim or satisfaction.

Gray Herb is chair of one Cabinet committee, and full member or ex-officio member of the other three. He is also on the powerful Board of Internal Economy, the executive committee that rules the operations of Parliament. His portfolio gives him access to great power as chief spook and cop.

In 1990, while serving as interim Leader of the Opposition, Gray Herb gave a keynote speech at the parliamentary press gallery dinner that fanned both reputation and fancy among journalists. He trained as a classical rather than avid pianist, and has gathered a wife called Sharon and two kids over the years.

THE HON. ANDRÉ OUELLET
Minister of Foreign Affairs

Department of Foreign Affairs and International Trade
- Canadian International Development Agency (CIDA)
- International Development Research Centre
- International Joint Commission
- International Centre for Human Rights and Democratic Development

With André, the adjectives come fast and furious. But they have rather a monotone

That kind of horrible, fratricidal war among such a formerly peaceful nation can only pain the world community.

No one likes to have the blood of innocents on their hands.

But, given my skills and the fact I'm in charge of passports, I doubt Parizeau and Bouchard will want to pay the price.

palette, the most innocuous being "crafty." A Liberal survivor from his first 1967 by-election victory, he has long assumed the mantle of Quebec lieutenant and political wise guy, unchallenged at present because of the weakness of Chrétien's Quebec choices and the sheer danger of getting André mad.

Ouellet was up to his shoulders in Turner's blood during the "dump Turner and stick him in a car trunk and leave him at Pearson" psycho-drama in the middle of the 1988 election.

Even someone as mild-mannered as the *Globe*'s Graham Fraser has no fear of summarizing Ouellet as a "sinister, manipulative back-room politician." He's always been a cold schemer, the Dave Dingwall (of whom more following) of the glorious Trudeau years and hatchet man for Marc Lalonde's management of the Quebec caucus. But his longevity and power base have assured him campaign co-chair status in recent election campaigns.

As minister of the former External Affairs, Ouellet has stayed out of trouble, though he has plumped rather brazenly for formerly bankrupt business guy Robert Campeau in the latter's attempt to over-develop Germany. And there are concerns he's been politicizing CIDA, though nothing has stuck to him yet. His natural habitat has always been Quebec, and this has taken more of his time than the affairs of the world. So far most of the paperwork coming out of his office focuses on the various Quebec cultural and performing arts groups being whisked about on special travel jaunts in service of Canada's foreign policy and standing.

THE HON. LLOYD AXWORTHY
Minister of Human Resources Development and Minister of Western Economic Diversification

Department of Human Resources Development
Department of Western Economic Diversification
- National Council on Welfare
- Labour Adjustment Review Board
- Canada Pension Plan Advisory Board

Poor Lloyd. A former Princeton scholar, and brother to the even brainier Tom Axworthy (a former adviser to Trudeau fondly referred to as "the fat guy"), he has been dunned. When curtly told his new power ministry would have a tiny support staff, the guy who once larded his old Transport portfolio with 75 ministerial staff should have seen it coming.

One expects Lloyd will be grabbed at any minute to be stuffed and displayed in the Saskatchewan Museum of Natural History as the last left-wing Liberal. He's been suffering through the portfolio equivalent of wearing a "kick me" sign. Since he's responsible for $70 billion of federal spending and 60% of the program budget, Cabinet colleagues bat him with socks of horseshit during meetings, and all those who've cashed – or were likely to cash – a

This isn't fun any more.

Hell, I never asked to be made the white knight for social spending. I thought it at least came with a decent staff.

I look to the right, and I see MacLaren, Massé, Martin, Manley, Eggs...the whole freakin' Cabinet and country.

I look to the left, and all I see are Warren Allmand and that Mary Walsh.

Neither beckons gently.

However, then again, the M boys are offering up one sweet mother of a pension scheme.

government support cheque have him ducking their wind-ups the rest of the time. The Liberal mania for bogus consultation right after the election was for him an unending foxtrot of public humiliation, abuse and macaroni showers. And then came Paul "Screw the Red Book" Martin, Jr., vaporizing Axworthy's tub of overdue social-program proposed reforms. What was left of his power and department was then whittled down even more to give Lucienne Robillard (see following) something to do in Cabinet.

When handed the social-policy mess, Axworthy quickly tried to reform targeted programs, saying silly things like "This is Actionville." He even moved quickly to snap up former *Financial Times* and *Globe* political columnist Giles Gherson, who had been offering Lloyd advice in the *Globe* before Jeffrey Simpson returned from sabbatical. But Axworthy was nobbled by consultation tours and his friends at the Cabinet table – and those *under* the Cabinet table, people like Eddie Goldenberg, who gnawed away at Axworthy's pins like a demented political rodent, making sure Axworthy wouldn't have the support to do anything, let alone *anything* that might piss off Quebec before the referendum.

The legendary patronage Santa for Western Canada won't last much longer. Nor will the former Liberal-style programs he still wants to champion.

Canada

Unemployment Insurance Reforms
Retraining Options 1

Proposed UI reforms contain many exciting proposals to enhance the lives of frequent users and Paul Martin, Jr. Here are some of the exciting, challenging ways those about to be trimmed off the public chequing account can improve their lot.

Personal Communication Technology Manager
Retraining chronic users of UI for a useful existence in the exciting field of communications. Retrainees will learn how to operate television, VCR, and stereo remotes for tired corporate managers, directors, and other professionals, as well as monitor telephone traffic, and develop call-waiting and call-forwarding skills.

Personal Perishable Consumables Technology Manager
Another retraining program offered by Human Resources, which provides retrainees with skills needed to operate and best utilize the advanced kitchen appliances and small food, preparation devices commonly found in the homes of tired corporate managers, directors, and other professionals.

Community Water Navigation Technology Manager
Former seasonal fishery workers will be taught to swim with a coloured blinking light strapped to their heads in busy or dangerous waterways.

For further information, please call Thomas D'Aquino.

Department of Human Resources Development | Ministère du Développement des ressore hérisson

THE HON. DAVID MICHAEL COLLENETTE

Minister of National Defence and Minister of Veterans Affairs

Department of National Defence
Department of Veterans Affairs
- Communications Security Establishment
- Emergency Preparedness Canada
- Bureau of Pensions Advocates
- Canadian Pension Commission
- Veterans Appeal Board
- Veterans Land Administration

Born in London, England, just after World War II, the ex–vice-president of Mandrake Management Consultants in Toronto is one of Chrétien's baldest cheerleaders. David paired with wife Penny back in 1975, and she is even tighter in the Chrétien circle of core loyalists, sitting in the PMO dishing out patronage jobs. They're touted as a power couple, but their parties in Ottawa's Highland Park have never had the sparkle or charm of those held by the neighbourhood's previous power duo – Richard and Sandra Gwyn. Both Collenettes served the Prime Minister in previous battles, though Penny was more active in the '84 leadership fight than David, who unsuccessfully tried to walk a line between Turner and Chrétien. In 1987 he was forced out as

As Commander-in-Chief...no, wait...that's Romeo...As Minister of Defence, I have a right to wear this.

It shows my sympathy with the poor grunts out there delivering pizza and learning how to be effective human shields.

Uh, and Penny loves a man in a uniform.

The Armed Forces: Rewarding part-time employment delivering pizzas

Build on your civilian career while you earn extra money working part-time for Jim's pizzeria, supplementing your regular pay. That's if you survive being de-layered and down-sized, shackled by some crazed Serb or Croat, or sodomized by some crazed former Airborne member.

Live this uniquely exciting experience. Work with interesting people. Enjoy varied opportunities for humiliation and frustration.

Dave, full-time Minister and part-time dork responsible for the Military.

CANADIAN
ARMED
FORCES

Canada

REGULAR AND UNLEADED

Liberal Party general secretary during the middle of the guerrilla campaign against Turner. Collenette, Dingwall, Goldenberg and Sergio Marchi (see following) are the names that most often squirt out when that dirty period is discussed.

David's loyalty, folded in with that of his wife, assured him a role in Cabinet when he returned to the government side of the Commons. Collenette was first elected in 1974, lost in the '79 Clark house-sit, and then made Cabinet in 1980 as Multiculturalism Minister. Years ago he tried to form a Walter Gordon dinner society, holding up the fervent Pearson-era nationalist as a hero. Now Gordon is considered an embarrassment – the current Cabinet never refers to him. David was out of Parliament for nine years until the 1993 sweep, and ascended to the Defence portfolio.

At Defence, Collenette has been part of the Cabinet troika – with Allan Rock and Brian Tobin – that the media has focused on since the election. Somalia, the Airborne, hazing, military college and base closures, Bosnia, and welfare soldiers have kept Collenette's shiny head on the tube. Loud and partisan in the Commons, the minister has a bit of madness about him when pumped up, though otherwise he settles into a comfortable funk of Roy MacLarenesque dullness (see following). He refused to take the advice of his Chief of Defence Staff not to disband the Airborne, but Collenette is still seen as going native in his department. Which means he'll likely be shuffled for his own safety. And the government's.

THE HON. ROY MACLAREN
Minister of International Trade

(shares some of Foreign Affairs offices)
- Export Development Corporation
- Canadian Secretariat (NAFTA)

Except for the Muldoon sweep in 1984, MacLaren has been in the Commons after every general election since 1979. Small media owner and author of a number of strange books, MacLaren looks like an extra from an Evelyn Waugh televison series or Merchant-Ivory film, and has a quiet, almost comatose media persona. Overeducated at UBC, Cambridge, and Harvard, and sporting a M. Div. from U of T, MacLaren wears Homburg hats, three-piece suits, bow-ties, and bicycle clips, all of which endear him to neo-conservatives, who have weaknesses for such things. And of course his reputation as Hard Right in a spineless Liberal caucus and Cabinet justifies their faith. Only the young fogies at the *Globe* could spin out an editorial calling him "an inspired, exciting choice for cabinet" and really, really mean it.

MacLaren supported NAFTA and Free Trade, but lost his Finance shadow position for favouring a consumption tax in 1989. It may seem he's an intellectual engine for the new Liberals, but in truth the party's philosophic retrofit has little to do with MacLaren's persuasive arguments at the Cabinet table. He has little presence in the current government, sitting on just one committee, travelling his own way wherever a delegation or conference catches his attention. He has no real department of his own, but utilizes parts of Ouellet's Foreign Affairs. Which works out just fine, because Ouellet isn't using much of it either. The PMO has adopted an amoral, wind-sniffing approach to international relations, so all foreign policy has been reduced to economics and trade. Which suits MacLaren and his growing collection of frequent-flyer points perfectly.

It is strongly rumoured that he has a jovial, moist and garrulous side, but it's something only Alethea, his three kids, and powerful Americans have seen.

THE HON. DAVID ANDERSON
Minister of National Revenue

Department of National Revenue

The former B.C. Liberal leader has been one of the select handful of ministers tagged by the media as in imminent danger of being shuffled off the big table. He was a last-minute choice for Cabinet, replacing Hedy Fry and Herb Dhaliwal, both ethnic choices from B.C. who didn't make it through Chrétien's ethical screening process. Somehow Anderson's $500,000 lawsuit against the federal government did, and the sight of a minister suing his own government made the media squeal with pleasure. Anderson had started the suit when the Tories cancelled his Turner patronage appointment to the Immigration Appeal Board in 1989, halfway through a 10-year term. He was quietly pressured into dropping a solid wrongful-dismissal suit for his fleeting ministerial perks and the chance to sit on two Cabinet committees.

Anderson is supposed to be political minister for B.C., yet he's not much of a player compared with an outsider like Ross Fitzpatrick, one of Chrétien's rich B.C. friends.

THE HON. RALPH E. GOODALE
Minister of Agriculture and Agri-Food

Department of Agriculture and Agri-Food
- Agricultural Stabilization Board
- National Farm Products Marketing Council
- Canadian Dairy Commission
- Canadian Wheat Board
- Farm Credit Corporation

Quiet and plain, Goodale hasn't made a noticeable mistake. A lawyer from a solidly urban Regina riding, he's flitted back and forth between federal and provincial politics for over 20 years. He's given himself over to the portfolio, and kept low. Considering the GATT furore about marketing boards, continued harassment from the Americans about agricultural exports, and Quebec's irritable dairy lobby, he's been very lucky.

Goodale has gradually earned some respect from select farmers. But he's certainly pissed off corn farmers in Ontario with his own Dingwaller of a move, closing down a chunk of the Central Experimental Farm in Ottawa and sending it to Saskatoon. Strangely, that transfer gives Saskatchewan a 6% increase in Agriculture and Agri-Food Canada research staff, while the department is cutting 28% of the positions, and 63% of those in eastern Ontario. Goodale has also moved the hog research program from outside Ottawa to Lennoxville, Quebec, spending millions for a new centre and leaving a relatively new one empty.

THE HON. DAVID DINGWALL
Minister of Public Works and Government Services and Minister responsible for the Atlantic Canada Opportunities Agency

Department of Public Works and Government Services
Atlantic Canada Opportunities Agency
- Canada Lands Company (CLC) Ltd.
- Canada Mortgage and Housing Corporation
- Canadian Commercial Corporation
- CLC (Mirabel) Ltd.
- CLC (Le Vieux-Port-de-Montréal) Ltd.
- Defence Construction (1951) Ltd.

- Harbourfront Corporation
- Royal Canadian Mint
- Canada Post Corporation
- Enterprise Cape Breton Corporation

The skinnier, scheming one of a brace of slap-heads close by Chrétien on the front bench, Dingwall is the Grit political boss for Atlantic Canada. His mother raised him in the basement of a Cape Breton school, where she worked as a janitor. He continued his schooling all the way to Dalhousie Law.

Davey was first elected to the Commons in 1980, and has been returned each election since. In 1982 he became parliamentary secretary to Marc Lalonde, and then Chrétien at Energy, Mines and Resources, where, like the great man's previous parliamentary secretary, Ron Irwin, Dingwall became a rabid Chrétien loyalist. In fact, the long gap of official party roles in his résumé from 1982 until 1989 is the result of his braying, black loyalty to Jean. Most of the pig-stickers and razor-chops aimed at Turner had Dingwall's prints on them. Or so the legend goes. As a result, Dingwall was frozen out by Turner and his besieged staff. Once Chrétien picked up what was left of the Liberal Party in 1990, revenge was sweet. Dave, ever the tough shit, gleefully changed the locks on Turner's Hill office when the latter gave Mulroney his support during the Gulf War. Dingwall then gave the new key to Sheila Copps.

During the Tory years, Dingwall was a preachy, shrill critic of Mulroney-era patronage excesses, something that will come back to haunt him and Chrétien. When appointed whip in 1990, Dingwall managed to beat the infamous Rat Pack into order, which, considering most were Chrétien loyalists, wasn't hard. But it cleaned up one of Turner's persistent media problems.

As the political heir to Senator Allan MacEachen's wizardry in the Maritimes, Dingwall doesn't have the same smarts or large moneybags. But by using the traditional billhooks and cudgels of politics – patronage and government contracts – Dingwallah has fashioned the East Coast into his own fiefdom. However, the combination of backroom hack and minister in charge of all government contracts was sure to explode. The only surprise was that it took as long as it did, when Dingwall was caught redirecting infrastructure money into his own riding. Dingwall's move to kill Toronto's Harbourfront was a real boner, but it was quickly forgotten after he did a U-turn on the issue.

In his department, Dingwall quickly changed the way advertising and polling are handled by the government. Worth about $80-$90 million a year, and the traditional way to pay off important party image-makers and pollsters, they've been centralized in Public Works by Dingwall.

Not a strong thinker, and not well enough connected to be an effective bagman, Dingwall is more of an unimaginative but unswerving officer carrying out orders. He's always interested in cutting a deal, but sticks to whatever overall goals have been identified. For example, when polls identified jobs and the economy as the major Canadian concerns, Dingwall managed Liberal questions in the House in the run-up to '93 to ensure most of the party's questions were about the economy. More chillingly, he knew the exact percentage: 87%. Scary. Cold. Efficient. Ruthless. Separated.

THE HON. RON IRWIN
Minister of Indian Affairs and Northern Development

Department of Indian Affairs and Northern Development
- Government of the Northwest Territories
- Government of the Yukon Territory
- Northern Canada Power Commission
- Northwest Territories Water Board
- Yukon Territory Water Board
- Canadian Polar Commission

In his rookie term, Irwin was Chrétien's parliamentary assistant at Justice in 1980. Long before Trudeau stepped down for the final time, Irwin eagerly sniffed the air for Chrétien's chances of gaining the leadership, and rounded up marginal caucus support. From then on, the colourful former Sault Ste. Marie mayor has been one of Chrétien's close hacks and touts. His folksy Northern Ontario ways, temper, and brutal frankness endear him to Chrétien, who has to work at keeping his unpolished language skills and populist tricks, which otherwise would be buffed up by endless rounds of golf and rich, powerful friends.

Like Sergio Marchi, Irwin is another damned accordionist, but has been relatively uncontroversial in his portfolio. After the Tory Tom Siddon, almost anything would have been welcomed with showers of flower petals and Inuit sculptures, and Irwin has enjoyed the goodwill of the Native clients. Outside the department, snooty, moist French columnist Michel Vastel pronounced Irwin a "moron" when he suggested aboriginals in Quebec have the right to stay in Canada. And Irwin enjoyed a few moments of fame when he called Reformer David Chatters a redneck. Other than championing some form of self-government for Natives, and hoping to gradually eliminate his department, Irwin meets and greets delegations and attends colourful ceremonies.

THE HON. BRIAN TOBIN
Minister of Fisheries and Oceans

Department of Fisheries and Oceans
- Fisheries Prices Support Board
- Fisheries Resources Conservation Council
- Freshwater Fish Marketing Corporation

Until the *Estai* went fishing for turbot, the most visible thing Brian Tobin had done since ascending to the ministry was shave his cheesy moustache. That effectively eradicated the last of his Rat Pack markings. Possessing an overarching political ego, a fetish for loud partisanship, and a growing love of the accoutrements of power, Tobin will eventually get an Order of Canada for his Turbot War performance. As sound bite and photo-op, it played brilliantly, allowing Martin's budget to escape scrutiny.

Tobin remains, er, aggressively aggressive, but has been robbed of opportunities to bark at inexperienced opposition members. For the first 18 months, however Tobin was stuck with a bad-news ministry, announcing or maintaining fishery closures and doling out a diminished compensation fund for the idle. He has mainly played to a Newf audience, so he thoroughly enjoyed the splash he made in the Turbot War. Other than a few nice video compilations and scrapbooks, Tobin has little to show for it all. He still has to finish digging a grave for a 500-year-old industry and somehow keep his client power-base from noticing the spade in his hands.

With the diminishing turbot euphoria, it's hopeless. Recent political spin has encouraged media speculation that Tobin will be shuffled to a new portfolio to utilize the bag of warm-fuzzies he gathered protecting ugly groundfish. Health or something politically sensitive has been

Fisheries and Oceans | Pêches d'avril et des Océans blue

Call for Tenders:
BT77734918743908983VC01212801824BC9 5-01886
Script Proposal for Next Ichthyographical Conflict

The Minister is accepting script or story proposals from the private sector for the next ministerial television extravaganza produced jointly by the department and the PMO for the Canadian viewing public. Documents must be neatly typed, in proper entertainment industry format, and be fresh-smelling.

Interested organizations and individuals should respond by December 31, 1995, for due consideration, and to ensure timing for following ratings period. Further information can be obtained by writing:

Hon. Brian Tobin
c/o David Dingwallah
Room 607, Confederation Building
Ottawa, Ontario
K1A 0A6
Phone: (613) 997-5421

All entries become property of the National Archives.

Canada

And looking at this chart here, you can see the poor state of migratory regeneration I mentioned in the previous seven graphs...

Zzzzzzzz...zzzz...zzzzz...zzzzzz...zzzzzzz...

Whu...am I Prime Minister yet?

mentioned. Unlikely. Given the few accomplishments of this Cabinet, Chrétien is not about to replace Tobin and put such a dangerous ministry in the hands of a new minister, struggling to learn all about the United Nations Office for Ocean Affairs and Law of the Sea, Northwest Atlantic Fisheries Organization, and "piscatorial pirates."

THE HON. JOYCE FAIRBAIRN
Leader of the Government in the Senate and Minister with special responsibility for Literacy

Joyce is the link between the two Houses of Parliament. A former aide to Trudeau in the '70s, and a former journalist, she was campaign co-chair in the last election. She enjoys a good reputation, and has helped out as an image consultant for Cabinet yahoos needing a bit of finishing. A quiet adviser and politically attuned, she has the unpleasant task of trying to keep the Tory majority in the Senate from hurting the government's legislative process, at least until enough Tory senators die or retire to give the Liberals control of the Upper House.

THE HON. SHEILA COPPS
Deputy Prime Minister and Minister of the Environment

Department of the Environment
• Canadian Evironmental Assessment Agency

A few husbands and make-overs have never really scrubbed away the Rat-Packer image, posing in black leather or scaring the bejeezus out of the Tories. Her political autobiography – *Nobody's Baby* – helped entrench her reputation – and clout – in the party. As well, her fluent French and womanly charms during her run for the federal leadership in 1990 got her noticed by the Chrétienophobic Quebec media. Things like calling herself the "ti-gosses," or testicles, of Hamilton did more for her than all the dweebs from Public Affairs International preaching voice-modulation ever could.

Sheila was ticketed for the Health portfolio until the last minute, though no one knows what collection of difficulties caused Chrétien to baulk. The post of Deputy Prime Minister is rather meaningless, and one of her early disappointments came in December 1993, when Chrétien disappeared for a while and Sheila publicly declared: "I'm in charge." She quickly learned she wasn't. She doesn't have the official office and sprawling staff of Muldoon's deputy, Don Mazankowski, which operated as a powerful parallel universe to the PMO. Copps is smart enough to now recognize that Gray Herb is the de facto DPM. She's hanging as a bit of window-dressing on Cabinet and is the beneficiary of a leadership peace-offering. If she had a more important portfolio, she'd be much happier. But then former leadership rivals aren't supposed to be.

She's recently started to settle in at Environment and, er, enjoy her portfolio. Though sexy for a while in the polls, Environment has been a non-starter since it was handed to Muldoon's friend Lucien Bouchard. In fact, Sheila's profile has become so low that *Frank* pulled her diary from its biweekly pages.

THE HON. SERGIO MARCHI
Minister of Citizenship and Immigration

Department of Citizenship and Immigration
• Immigration and Refugee Board

The fact that Sergio "Jim" Marchi has had no real-world experience outside of politics hasn't hurt him. In fact, little has. Though he has a reputation for gleeful political rabbit-punching and pig-sticking, earned during the bloody, prolonged game of Mumblety-Peg using Turner's back, it hasn't surfaced as a minister. He's been a solid Chrétien fixer, loyalist, and wiseguy for over a decade.

He was born in Argentina of Italian parents, and has the haunting look of that Luffwaffe pilot in Hollywood movies who always climbs out of a downed plane and calmly lights up a smoke. After settling in Alberta, the Marchi clan moved on to Toronto, where Sergio learned to play the accordion and be a North York alderman. When he was just out of York University, his reputation as an organizer and fixer earned him the call to fly up to the heavily Italian Sault Ste. Marie and run Ron Irwin's 1980 federal campaign. Marchi then followed Irwin to Ottawa, and a year later jumped to become assistant economic advisor to Multiculturalism Minister Jim Fleming.

Marchi clawed his own way to the Commons in 1984, and fell in with Rat-Packers Nunziata, Copps, Tobin, and Don Boudria. When the Chrétienists finally got rid of Turner, Marchi and Tobin gave their energies over to the election-readiness committee. Both worked closely with Chrétien and other key loyalists on organization and strategy. Relaxing after one session at the Ping-Pong table, Chrétien beat Marchi and Tobin single-handedly, which probably alone cinched their seats at the Cabinet table.

Though mainly considered political muscle and gamesman, Marchi has gathered a staff that has done a good job briefing and packaging him. He even grabbed Judy Morrison, the former host of CBC's *The House*, when she was elbowed out by Jason Moscovitz. That and ineffective opposition have kept Marchi intact,

Mr. Speaker, sustainable immigration is a prime concern of this minister, and this government.

To propose immigration policies that sustain us in government, and knock out a big plank of Reform is absolutely this minister's...

ooooh, ooooh...jammed finger jammed finger jammed finger.

despite the early political row over criminal immigrants, and Reform-inspired changes to immigration policy.

THE HON. JOHN MANLEY
Minister of Industry
Department of Industry
- Cape Breton Development Corporation (DEVCO)
- Statistics Canada
- Competition Tribunal
- Copyright Board
- Standards Council of Canada
- Canadian Space Agency
- Natural Sciences and Engineering Research Council
- National Research Council
- Social Sciences and Humanities Research Council
- Federal Business Development Bank

John Manley – one of the legendary "Four Ms" (Martin, Massé, and MacLaren are the others) – has become junior minister to Martin by default. The most exciting thing he's done is handle the seal of Canada at the end of the Cabinet swearing-in. Funny, well-liked, and earnest, the devout Anglican and golfer has damn near everyone convinced he's a nice guy. Like Allan Rock, he's someone who went into politics to make things better.

A tax lawyer out of the University of Ottawa, Manley has lived in the capital all his life. His CV is topped up with impressive stuff, like being Bora Laskin's clerk and the kid chair of the Ottawa-Carleton Board of Trade. Like most of his "fellow Ms," if not the whole Cabinet, he's more "blue grit" than "true grit," but then the latter brings only madness and frustration. Ask Axworthy or Warren Allmand.

Manley got the portfolio Paul Martin really wanted, a power-potential department cobbled together from bits of five others. But C. D. Howe, Manley ain't, though he uses the old Liberal industry czar's desk. The new minister was supposed to bring in a host of programs and initiatives based on the Red Book to pro-

No, I'm perfectly comfortable with Cabinet's DTH satellite policy.

Why, do I look uncomfortable with it?

Should I look uncomfortable with it?

mote small businesses and companies, research and development, and export growth. But after Martin so forcefully scuttled his own creation with his "Screw the Red Book!" screeches to Finance Department flunkies, the promises remain as only folk memories.

Manley's responsibility to clean up lobbying was effectively taken over by Chrétien, who did less than expected. And Manley's one major accomplishment, an internal trade agreement reached in July 1994, was really the conclusion of Tory negotiatons on a Tory initiative. Manley even left the structure and personnel alone when he took over, not changing a hair on anyone's head. Things like that have made it easier to believe that the Muldoon and Campbell Tories didn't die in 1993: they were just reincarnated as Chrétien's Cabinet.

A nice, really nice guy, but he's spinning his wheels, and the wheels of industry.

NRC-CNRC

NRC – Canada's only R&D organization – helps its industry partners become stronger global competitors by doing the research they should if they weren't so short-sighted and greedy. Currently, NRC uses AC, but has the capability to use DC off car batteries for really complicated experiments. And we're looking for Research Officers who can help further our record of excellence.

Process Technology

(Two positions)
Two-year term: Reference EC-95-000000002.GM

The Process Technology Program is in its twenty-third exciting year, and is designed to develop a response to the process in American Process Cheese foods. The key discipline to be applied is chemical engineering.

Position requirements: Ph.D. in chemical engineering or a Queen's political studies degree, or an equivalent combination of education and handwritten certificate from Jag Bhaduria. The language requirement for both positions is either English or French. A security screening is required.

To explore one of these opportunities, send your application to: John Manley, Recruitment and Staffing Section, MININD, Ottawa K1A 0H5

National Research Council Canada | Conseil national de rechigneux Canada | Canada

THE HON. DIANE MARLEAU
Minister of Health

Department of Health
- Canadian Centre on Substance Abuse
- Medical Research Council
- Patented Medicine Prices Review Board
- National Advisory Council on Aging
- Hazardous Materials Information Review Commission

Diane was marked by the media "certain-to-be-shuffled-soon" even before the ink was dry on her oaths of Cabinet office in 1993. Immediately beset by a national rage for tobacco smuggling, her weak, uncertain performance only shot up the odds against her hanging on. But she has. She was supposed to get something uncontroversial like Revenue, but Chrétien was forced to do some last-minute reshuffling before the Cabinet was set, and the stolidly loyal Marleau ended up in a tumbril and directed to the Tunney's Pasture Health bureaucracy.

A former Sudbury secretary, alderman, and regional councillor, she even owned a restaurant before rolling into the Commons in 1988. She has three kids, a wealthy husband who recently cashed in a small fortune in media holdings, and a reputation for thinking herself smarter than she is. Considered right of centre, with no real beliefs, she tried to cultivate an image of being a Northern Ontario Maggie Thatcher.

Through her missteps, confused bravado, and a fog of platitudes and emptiness, she's presided over a withering health-care system, yet blames the media, who cast her as a "dumb broad from Kirkland Lake," for her problems – a sure sign of weakness and danger. Billions of dollars lost in cigarette-tax revenue, plain packaging, a toothless Canada Health Act, and the misappropriation of Elsie Wayne's likeness are just smoke plumes of a raging furnace of intense underperformance that have laid waste to a traditional Liberal power centre.

No, I have it directly from the Prime Minister. He's made it very clear to my colleagues.

Federal support for health care is as solid as my Cabinet seat.

Let me try to rephrase that.

THE HON. PAUL MARTIN
Minister of Finance and Minister responsible for the Federal Office of Regional Development – Quebec

Department of Finance
FORD–Q

- Bank of Canada
- Canada Deposit Insurance Corporation
- Canada Development Investment Corporation
- Canadian International Trade Tribunal
- Office of the Superintendent of Financial Institutions
- Procurement Review Board

He's the son of Paul Martin, Sr., a legend in the dusty annals of liberal Liberals, and the godfather of Canadian social spending. Junior constantly says he is his father's son in speeches, budget preambles, and probably the mirror every morning. But he doth protest too much. He has

No, I am very much my father's son. The legacy he helped build is precisely the one I see shackling businesses everywhere.

I mean, that helps us from the trough at the bottom of a business cycle.

As my father helped smother us in a cradle-to-grave economic wet blanket...

I mean, fed us with the rightful fruits of a civilized society...in the same way my 3% of GDP is the ultimate social program...

...one that goes a great way to ensuring the orderly wrap-up of the earlier ones.

(If I cross all my toes any harder and longer, I'm gonna throw my damn hip out.)

a different view of the world and Canada than his father did – as does Chrétien the Power Corp. initiate compared with Chrétien the unilingual Shawinigan populist. While Chrétien is at peace with his duality, and has admitted as much in *Straight from the Heart*, Martin, Jr., stammers with Oedipal anxiety over his. It's funny and sad.

The psychological pressure on Martin, Jr., could be seen as a brilliant manipulation by the Chrétien inner circle. When Paul was denied his original request to be made the new C.D. Howe, and convinced to take Finance, it effectively limited Martin's reputation. And since Chrétien, almost devoid of policy and guiding principles, grafted Martin's leadership program to stand in for his own, this was no small consideration. A former leadership rival with a power base and growing reputation could be political hell. Ask Joe Clark or John Turner. Back in February 1991, Martin could have caused a debilitating war in the Liberal caucus when he announced there was policy vacuum that needed filling. Instead, he became the filling.

But at a cost. Since the election he has been mercilessly, humorously, but unfairly ripped apart by Dalton Camp in the *Toronto Star*. More damaging is Martin's uncanny ability to look and sound like the stunned airline navigator Howard Borden on the old Bob Newhart show. Ultimately more damaging was Ron Graham's February 1995 *ROB Magazine* profile, which described Martin as screaming at his bureaucrats, "Screw the Red Book!" That clinched him as another cynical, egotistical politician running away from promises. All the Finance bureaucrats did to earn Martin's abuse was, like most Canadians, to take Martin the policy guru at his word, and try to stick to the Grit script. Wrong answer. But to be honest, how could a businessman whose net worth is easily $30 million understand how close to the edge many Canadians are, and why so many responded so favourably to the Red Book?

Martin, like Chrétien, Mulroney, and almost every Quebec pol on the make, has impeccable connections to Paul Desmarais and Power Corp. Though he started at Power before Desmarais bought it, Martin stayed on for more than 13 years after Desmarais took control, finally purchasing Power's transport conglomerate, CSL Group Inc. Martin did turn it around brilliantly, and crawled out from under a pile of debt. But he still retains his ownership of CSL, a company with a number of dealings with Canadian agencies. His potential for an embarrassing conflict of interest is the highest of any recent Cabinet minister. Though he has turned over day-to-day control to a lawyer at Canada Trust Co., the extent and value of his corporate holdings make any fiscal or tax policy an indirect conflict. And the honour and utility of keeping politicians away from their businesses was brought into question when Ontario's Lieutenant-Governor, Hal Jackman, had to be warned repeatedly to stay away from his National Trustco Inc. by federal ethics pooh-bah Howard Wilson. When Jackman snapped that "you can't own that amount of stock without accepting some sort of responsibility," he raised an argument that could resonate with the owner of CSL. Wilson hopes Martin will be better at restraining himself from temptation.

THE HON. DOUGLAS YOUNG
Minister of Transport

Department of Transport
- Canada Ports Corporation
- Canadian National Railway Company
- Canarctic Shipping Company Ltd.
- Civil Aviation Tribunal
- Grain Transportation Agency
- Jacques Cartier and Champlain Bridges Inc.
- Laurentian Pilotage Authority
- Marine Atlantic Inc.
- National Transportation Agency
- St. Lawrence Seaway Authority
- VIA Rail Canada Inc.

Another lawyer in Cabinet, Young evolved from the New Brunswick legislature and leadership of the provincial Liberal Party, first standing upright in the 1988 federal election. Highly partisan by nature, he's enjoyed moments of theatre in the House, but has for the most part disappeared from public view – quite an accomplishment, given the stalling of the Pearson Airport bill, the privatization of the CNR, and the termination of Canadian transport subsidies. Young is quietly managing his portfolio, and is considered to be well outside the Cabinet power circle.

Transport Canada **Airports** | Transports Canada **Aéroports**

TORONTO – LESTER B. PEARSON INTERNATIONAL AIRPORT
PEST AND SENATE CONTROL SERVICES
80 Wellington Street
Ottawa, Ontario
K1A 0A2

SEALED TENDERS for the project listed in the newspapers and addressed to Pest and Senate Control Services, 80 Wellington Street, and in the pre-addressed tender envelope (be gentle) will be received up to tee-time, most days, before the specified Senate report is due.

TENDER NO. PMO-95-99943	SENATE ABATEMENT, TERMINATE ONE INTRANSIGENT BUNCH OF TORIES DERAILING THE PEARSON PRIVATIZATION DIS-AGREEMENT
DEPOSIT: 10 cents a bottle	CHEQUE PAYABLE TO RECEIVER GENERAL FOR CANADA
BRIEFS	PLEASE CHANGE THEM AND BOXERS DAILY.

PMO does not bind itself to accepting the lowest or any tender. Or to anything in the Red Book.

Canada

CABINET

THE HON. MICHEL DUPUY
Minister of Canadian Heritage

Department of Canadian Heritage
- Canada Council
- Canadian Broadcasting Corporation
- Canadian Radio-television and Telecommunications Commission
- National Archives of Canada
- National Arts Centre Corporation
- National Film Board
- National Library of Canada
- Telefilm Canada
- Canadian Museum of Civilization
- Canadian Museum of Nature
- National Gallery of Canada
- National Museum of Science and Technology
- National Capital Commission
- National Battlefields Commission
- Canadian Cultural Property Export Review Board
- Canadian Advisory Council on the Status of Women
- Public Service Commission

National Capital
Commission

TENDER CALL

P04577291839848BX129938-9592-1c
Tulip Bulb Survey
Ottawa/Hull

Sealed tenders corresponding to the title projects and addressed to:

Senior Contract Officer
Procurement Management Services
National Capital Commission
c/o Hon. David Dingwallah
Room 607, Confederation Building
Ottawa, Ontario
K1A 0A6
Phone: (613) 997-5421
cc Michel Dupuy

were received until yesterday, local time.

Tender documents can be purchased at a refundable cost of $100 per tender package and dinner ticket. Payment, in cash, should be made at the door.

The lowest or any tender not necessarily accepted by the minister.

Canada

A former diplomat, with postings in France and at the UN, and considered a capable public servant, Dupuy has been second only to Marleau in shuffle pools that began almost as soon as the swearing-in ended. He was one of many select advisers tutoring Chrétien prior to the 1990 leadership bid, and so loyalty as well as a lack of Quebec bench-strength has kept Dupuy at the table long after most anyone else would have been heaved. The convoluted explanations during the Ginn Publishing sell-off – or sell-out – were merely comic, compared with Dupuy's unsuccessful lobbying of the CRTC – one of his own ministerial responsibilities – on behalf of a constituent. Although this gaffe was immediately excused as "an honest mistake," Dupuy should have resigned, even if for a short time. Instead, he's continued to appear ineffectual in both the Seagrams acquisition coincidence and the Power DirecTV decision.

Though not looking like a career politician can be a positive blessing, Dupuy has the tangible mien of another time about him. Aping a partisanship completely foreign to his nature, he looks baffled – particularly because he's been scrambling to defend the indefensible. It's a shame, but Dupuy's performance and treatment will probably do more to keep non-lawyers out of Ottawa than the alleged low pay.

CRTC Canada

Decision

Decision 95-0000000000000001b. **PowerDirecTV Inc. DTH Service** The Canadian Radio-television and Telecommunications Commission has decided, after many glaring lapses of good judgement and years of appeasement, to pick a fight with our political masters. Call it populism. Call it opportunism. Call it boredom on Keith Spicer's part. Just don't call it a stand on principle, because we and you both know better.

Those in the Prime Minister's Office who wish to appeal this decision can do so by couriering a formal objection, wedding videos of André and France, personal mementos of John Rae, audited statements of campaign contributions from Power Corp., and anything else of relevance.

To obtain CRTC documents, contact the CRTC at: Ottawa-Hull (819) 997-2429. Or the Prime Minister's Ethics Counsellor at (613) 995-6852. To obtain silly comments from the CRTC chair, all you have to do is ask.

Canadian Radio-Television and Telecommunications Commission | Conseil de canadienne bon ton Keith Spicer

THE HON. ARTHUR C. EGGLETON
President of the Treasury Board and Minister responsible for Infrastructure
Treasury Board Secretariat

An accountant by profession and temperament, he is happily married to his second wife, Brenda, but relaxes when time permits by hitting the road with

...hmmmmmmmmmmm...

...hmmmmmmmmmmmmmmm.

No, I'm sure. MacLaren's much duller than I am.

triathlon training partner Betty Disero, the Toronto city councillor.

The earnest, athletic Eggleton has been true to himself since becoming an accountant for Volvo when everyone else was having fun in the 1960s. As mayor of Toronto for an amazing 11 years, he was prone to sleeping in barber chairs, at his own birthday in 1988, and anytime the clock struck eleven. He is a man of uncomplicated principles, always ready to make a deal.

Bean-counter for this ministry, Eggs controls the purse strings of program spending. Chrétien once served the same role, and relishes the rather fanciful notion that he was a feared Dr. No. Eggleton also has control over the $6-billion infrastructure program with which the Liberals were going to rebuild the economy. Now the plan has been taffy-pulled out an extra few years, substantially diminishing its initial cost and effectiveness, but it'll still allow Chrétien to say they kept their promise.

That kind of money sloshing around raised the eyebrows of those who still couldn't believe that the former pro-development mayor who crept out of scandal-ridden Toronto without a black mark on him would be lucky twice. But so far a cursory check of the divvying of Infra money has found only Dingwallah's fingerprints.

Spooky points for Reformers: Eggs was a former World Bank consultant and is a Catholic convert.

THE HON. MARCEL MASSÉ
President of the Queen's Privy Council for Canada, Minister of Intergovernmental Affairs and Minister responsible for Public Service Renewal

- Public Service Staff Relations Board
- Canadian Transportation Accident Investigation and Safety Board

A Rhodes Scholar, former Clerk of the Privy Council, and twice president of the Canadian International Development Agency, Massé was considered a brilliant civil servant and a great catch by the Liberals when he bailed out of the public service. Both Massé and Michel Dupuy (another former public servant) have unfortunate appearances that could be dropped plausibly, if not comfortably, into any St. Laurent–era Cabinet photo.

The grafting of public servants onto Liberal Cabinet seats hasn't been a great success. Massé doesn't look quite as bad as Dupuy, but he's had a few amusing missteps as minister. Barely sworn in, he was embarrassed by running up $173,000 worth of government jet time for political speeches in Boston and New Orleans. And a frank comment that health costs would have to be pared by 20% gave everyone – especially Marleau and the PMO – a severe attack of the willies.

Since then, Marcel has kept away from scrums. He's a Cabinet committee workhorse, serving as vice-chair on Social Development Policy, and one of only four ministers on Economic Development Policy. Massé also sits on Treasury Board. PCO secrecy makes it hard to determine how much of a power he is in moving the tons of paper through Cabinet, and the same impediment blocks analysis of his federalist scheming as President of the Queen's Privy Council. And as Intergovernmental Affairs Minister, Massé and his newly imported helpmate, Lucienne Robillard, were supposed to revive the spark in the federalist cause, but so far it seems they're still vainly rubbing sticks.

Only as Minister responsible for Public Service Renewal, or rather "Public Service Removal," has Massé been detected, setting Chrétien's former PCO Dobermann David Zussman loose on all government departments to identify the deadwood. The public service can expect a good old Roman-style decimation in their ranks, if not worse, if Martin needs it.

Canada

PUBLIC SERVICE REMOVAL

Beginning November 30, 1995, under new guidelines from the Hon. Marcel Massé, President of the Queen's Privy Council for Canada, Minister of Intergovernmental Affairs, and Minister responsible for Public Service Removal, surplus Public Service of Canada assets will be collected only on alternate Thursdays.

Managers must place surplus assets in the appropriate recycle or retraining box by 10 a.m. the day of collection for pick-up by Human Resources Development for prompt, courteous disposal. Use of distributed bio-hazard bags is mandatory.

Public Service assets improperly placed in recycle or retraining boxes without completed paperwork or after office parties will result in the return of same assets at the next scheduled collection.

For further information or position status, contact:

The Minister for Public Service Removal
155 Queen Street
Ottawa, Ontario K1A 0A6
Or call: (613) 943-1838

Public Service Commission of Canada

Commission de la fafoin poqué du Canada

THE HON. ANNE MCLELLAN
Minister of Natural Resources

Department of Natural Resouces
- Atomic Energy Control Board
- Atomic Energy of Canada Ltd.
- Canada-Newfoundland Offshore Petroleum Board
- National Energy Board
- Canada-Nova Scotia Offshore Petroleum Board
- Northern Pipeline Agency

A last-minute Cabinet inclusion when a recount gave her a single-digit majority in the riding of Edmonton Northwest, the constitutional law professor is one of the Cabinet's low-profile second members. The rookie politician has been ineffectually spinning her intellectual wheels in a portfolio that doesn't make sense for her. If she was from the oilpatch or Calgary, maybe it would. She's done good work in Cabinet committees, she serves as vice-chair for Economic Development Policy – and uses her legal wits among the depressing forlorn-hopes sitting with her on the Special Committee of Council, reviewing legislative clauses.

The political minister for Alberta, and relatively harmless.

THE HON. ALLAN ROCK
Minister of Justice and Attorney General of Canada

Department of Justice and Attorney General of Canada
- Canadian Human Rights Commission
- Offices of the Information and Privacy Commissioners
- Office of the Commissioner of Federal Judicial Affairs

A prime minister in a hurry, Allan Rock has been the irritatingly smug face of the government's nominally liberal programs. Gun registration, same-sex benefits, young offenders, hate crimes, doctor-assisted suicide, family support payments: all have turned the supposedly shy Toronto lawyer and former treasurer of the Law Society of Upper Canada into a media beast. He has yet to meet a microphone he doesn't like, and in his zest to push his legislative fixes or contain damage, he's wallowed in some questionable pools of logic and argument. All this has somewhat lessened the early claims he made that he'd do things differently, and help (like, uh, Preston Manning, wasn't it?) transform the Commons into a more business like, non-partisan, effective place.

A star candidate in '93, complete with the Keith Davey stamp of approval,

I think I once again speak for all Canadians when I say we deserve peace and security.

Yet my good, simple efforts have met a brick wall of hostility. People register this anger with me every day.

AHA! If you people are willing to register your opinions with a politician, then surely you can register your silly guns with him.

I'm sorry. I think my zealous desire to solve all our problems has pushed me over the line towards insults and disrespect.

My only goal is to listen to the voices, and tapestrize them into a harmony of happy song drowning out the losers.

And if that fails, I crush, I crush your silly Reform heads atop your tiny red necks.

Rock filled newspapers with glowing profiles and ActionMan photos. Some of the most memorable glimpses were provided by the *Globe*'s normally sensible Susan Delacourt, who described a life-force of honesty and innocence in a handsome man who just wanted to do good. Easily taking Michael Wilson's old riding of Etobicoke Centre, Rock was easily rewarded with a Cabinet post.

For a government with little to show for its first few years but a few Spanish fishing nets and *Wall Street Journal* editorials, Rock's controversial bills have been important, creating the impression of some sort of government momentum, or life. They're the expensive, really pointless feel-good stuff salvaged from the Red Book, the only liberal togs Chrétien's wonks have in the tickle-trunk. Handling them all has placed enormous pressure on the rookie, and the load will hurt him. Unlike many of his Cabinet colleagues, who hit the road for public-relations reasons, Rock is considered a true consultation geek and conciliation freak, but he's ushered bills that have created uncompromising camps.

A long-distance runner who still seeks revenge on Supreme Court judge John Sopinka for beating him in races almost two decades ago, Rock is really in training for the leadership marathon. As a Catholic, English (but bilingual) lawyer, with a lawyer wife called Debbie and four kids, he's certainly well constructed, having the necessary parts to be the next Liberal leader. But with no power base of his own in Quebec, he'd depend on the kindness of strangers.

THE HON. LUCIENNE ROBILLARD
Minister of Labour

(shares some of Human Resources offices)
- Canada Labour Relations Board
- Canadian Centre for Occupational Health and Safety
- Merchant Seamen Compensation Board
- Canadian Artists and Producers Professional Relations Tribunal

Heralded as a rising star and hand-picked by Chrétien to give some sex appeal to the federalist cause, she has yet to peep over the horizon. Lucienne was elected in February 1995 in a by-election, when a seat was voluntarily vacated by grit David Berger. Robillard was a respected minister in the Quebec Liberal party, and became available after losing her seat in the 1994 provincial election. Thought to be a soft nationalist, and without political affiliation until 1989, she is a bit of an unknown federalist entity, but no one in charge seems worried.

In a reasonably blatant attempt to cut into the media's fascination with Lucien Bouchard's return to the Commons after his amputation, Robillard was theatrically escorted into the House as a new MP by Chrétien and Ouellet. Ouellet, of course, remains firmly in control as Quebec lieutenant, but Robillard's arrival was a bit of a slight to charisma-less Marcel Massé, who still holds the Intergovernmental Affairs portfolio. Robillard's department was cut from Axworthy's, and is just the latest of many embarrassments Lloyd has suffered in Cabinet. But the portfolio was joy for Diane Marleau. Robillard's previous experience with Quebec's Health and Education portfolios fuelled speculation that Diane would finally get the hook.

THE HON. JON GERRARD
Secretary of State (Science, Research and Development)

A pediatric hematologist and fomer professor of pediatrics, Gerrard is a scientist and intellectual in a Cabinet more comfortable with instinct. Full marks for a spirit of public service. Good odds against making the front bench.

THE HON. FERNAND ROBICHAUD

Secretary of State (Agriculture and Agri-Food, Fisheries and Oceans)

(Who dat? – ed.)

THE HON. SHEILA FINESTONE

Secretary of State (Multiculturalism, Status of Women)

Tiny little Sheila has sat in the House, dressed in the style her constituents in Mont Royal expect, since 1984. She's probably best known as the feisty critic of Tory communications policies during the Muldoon years, when she kept up a lonely counter-attack on philistinism. But she was passed over for the new Heritage portfolio when Chrétien needed stronger Quebec representation in the ministry. Dupuy's performance must bring flutters of expectation to her heart. However, Chrétien's Quebec balance would be uncomfortably low without Michel.

THE HON. LAWRENCE MACAULAY

Secretary of State (Veterans)

A P.E.I. farmer in his second term in the Commons. Er, that's about it.

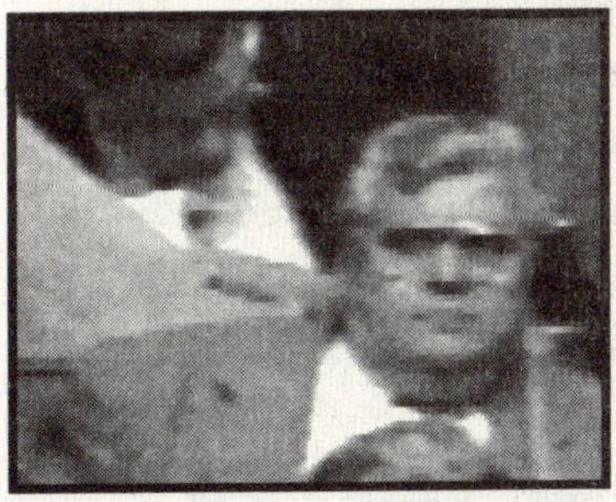

THE HON. ALFONSO GAGLIANO

Secretary of State (Parliamentary Affairs) and Deputy Leader of the Government in the House of Commons

Originally Government whip, Gagliano was kicked upstairs in 1994 after quickly introducing an austerity program for MPs. No redecorating, no free shoeshines or picture framing, a 70% cut in barbers' and user fees, and closer monitoring of other perks. Like Gray Herb, Gagliano sits on the Board of Internal Economy, the powerful Commons committee that runs the physical plant of Parliament. Alfonso's been in the House for over a decade, and has accumulated a bag of tricks and valuable information that makes managing people much easier. Though he revels in his role as confessor, consultant, and cappuccino jockey to members, no one has dared cross him.

THE HON. CHRISTINE STEWART
Secretary of State (Latin America and Africa)

Perky but relatively harmless.

THE HON. DOUGLAS PETERS
Secretary of State (International Financial Development)

A brainy Queen's B.Comm and University of Pennsylvania Ph.D. from Toronto, Peters tools along in the background with the charismatic Roy MacLaren, looking at numbers and trends. Topped to the gills with personality and royal jelly like MacLaren, Peters has a good chance of hitting the front, given the amount of seating reserved for conservative, responsible bean-counters. But someone will have to really screw up or die first.

THE HON. ETHEL BLONDIN-ANDREW
Secretary of State (Training and Youth)

The MP for Western Arctic first came to the House in 1988. She's received a fair amount of favourable media coverage, and is generally liked and considered hard-working. Unfortunately the second tier is probably as high as she'll go, barring the outbreak of plague in the front benches.

THE HON. RAYMOND CHAN
Secretary of State (Asia-Pacific)

Chan emigrated from Hong Kong over 26 years ago, and speaks Mandarin and Cantonese. Though he studied engineering, he opened a Chinese restaurant, which he sold in 1989, and eventually got drawn into politics. Chan doesn't exactly know why, though he's said human-rights abuses in China – especially the massacre in Tiananmen Square – finally got him active. Unfortunately we have no idea how he squares his motivational sense of outrage with the more forgiving attitude of his government.

The Bank of Canada

The Bank of Canada is a fixture on Wellington Street, Canada's main street of power. Its psychic presence can be felt down the middle of the city and out to the 'burbs, through the asphalt march of Bank Street. It began life as a private enterprise in 1934. Two years later, the Liberals started nationalizing it. By 1950, it finally replaced the other bank notes floating around Canada with its own. The Bank's most visible role is still issuing the paper and metal we use. It designs the look of our money, hoards our precious metals and foreign-currencies reserves, runs the Canada Savings Bond campaign, and oversees operation of commercial banks.

In the somewhat intentionally eye-glazing world of economics (ignorance breeds peace), the Bank of Canada controls and closely monitors different categories of money supply, or the amount of cash and credit sloshing around the system.

DISCOVER

the

CURRENCY

MUSEUM

BANK OF CANADA

BANK OF CANADA
245 SPARKS STREET
OTTAWA, ONTARIO

Free admission on Tuesday because we're all too busy upstairs setting the trend-setting Bank of Canada rate you'll see on the news when you get home.

Relive great moments in history by tracing the development of Tight Money and Zero Inflation policy in Canada. Discover the amazing differences between John Crow and Gordon Thiessen as you're surrounded by a huge 3-D graph plotting the Bank Rate fluctuations for the last 13 years. Or you can waste your time looking at the old scraps of paper, metal, bone, shell, glass beads, fish hooks, teeth, grain, cattle, cocoa beans and playing cards people once believed fiscally secure. Or learn how to counterfeit or transfer money to the Cayman Islands.

Make you next outing an expensive one – discover the Currency Museum.

Offer not valid in an Independent Quebec.

On Tuesday the Bank of Canada conducts an auction of Treasury bills. When it buys T-bills, the Bank tosses hundreds of millions of bucks into the system, and interest rates usually drop by 100ths of a percent. When it sells T-bills, the Bank vacuums up cash, and interest rates usually rise by 100ths of a percent. That's about as amusing as the place gets.

Because these rises and falls are regular, and easily obtained, the media trumpets them as if they meant something – the thick lines on their graphs seem ominous and important. The rate is a barometer of economic direction, or a Band-Aid to stop currency speculators. But in theory it hasn't much bearing on what average Canadians fork over as interest on a number of commercial transactions. We've been conditioned to think that rate-setting is important, so now it is.

Running the show is the Governor, whose signature guarantees our bills are at least worth the paper they're printed on. Governors are appointed as overseers, like Joseph's dreams in Egypt, for seven-year terms. We force them to subsist on a meagre $250,000 a year, unless we want done of them, in which case we pony up a year's salary as a parting gift, and drop another $30,000 for a three-city, six-event going-away tour that passes out gold-plated Whip Inflation Now buttons bought at a White House garage sale. Crow is an expensive dish to fix properly. Fortunately for the Liberals, they killed two birds with one stone: getting rid of the (John) Crow that set the Rate, and the Crow (Rate) that subsidized grain farmers. People were so happy to see the end of the former, they didn't notice Doug Young's doing away with the latter.

The current guv is a lifer in the Bank, a quiet Saskatchewan fellow called Gordon Thiessen. He reached an agreement with Paul Martin, Jr., to keep the Bank's war on inflation at around the 3% number the Finance Minister is strangely attracted to. And Thiessen was forced to axe some sizeable pay increases around 234 Wellington, showing a flair for public relations that'll force him to watch his back while mingling with Bank directors and underlings if he tries that kind of stunt again. As chairman of the board of directors, CEO of the Bank, and adviser to the Finance Minister, he has power most mandarin wannabes dare not whisper of. The senior deputy guv, the position Thiessen held prior to becoming guv, also signs our bills, and has almost as much power as his boss, especially when the guv phones in sick.

Directors of the Bank of Canada

You have no chance of influencing Bank policy. The institution is secretive, even by Ottawa standards. But the board of directors convenes a number of times each year to meet with Bank staff; rubber-stamp the appropriate documents; and fill them in on regional gripes, fears, and wishes. Scan business class, the local airport VIP lounge, or the better restaurants when seeking a chance to buttonhole your regional director with your suggestions.

Fernand G. Dubé, Dubé & Dubé, Campbellton, N.B.

Joseph Kruger II, Chairman & CEO Kruger Inc., Montreal, Que.

Harold H. MacKay, Q.C., Managing Partner MacPherson Leslie & Tyerman, Regina, Sask.

Donald J. Matthews, Chairman Matthews Construction Canada Inc., Brampton, Ont.

Judith Maxwell, President CPRN Inc., Ottawa, Ont.

James S. Palmer, Q.C., Chairman Burnet, Duckworth & Palmer, Calgary, Alta.

Charles Pelletier, F.C.A., Caron Bélanger Ernst & Young, Quebec City, Que.

Donald S. Reimer, Chairman, President & CEO Reimer Express Enterprises, Winnipeg, Man.

Barbara F. Stevenson, Q.C., Carr, Stevenson & MacKay, Charlottetown, P.E.I.

The Canadian Dollar

The Canadian peso or loonie is the basic unit of commerce in Canada. Everyone gets paid in it, except professional baseball players. And everyone uses it, except Canadian press lords.

The single dollar is called a "loonie" because of the bizarre monetary policies of former Bank of Canada governor John Crow. In recognition of the epithet, Crow selected a lone Canadian loon swimming against the current as the image on the eleven-sided coin when the familiar trade canoe of the old dollar coins couldn't be used because Bank and Royal Mint flunkies lost the dies.

Americans may still enjoy using "sound as a dollar" to describe stability, but Canadians have increasingly taken to hoarding Club Z points and Canadian Tire money as a way of frustrating international money speculators.

The Currency Museum

Old dollars of all types can be found in the Currency Museum, located on the ground floor of the Bank of Canada. While not as impressive as the Bank of England's museum in London, it's a good way to kill an hour or two. You can see the display showing the comical "worth" of Canadian and world denominations. But go on Free Tuesdays, the day officials upstairs are busy hoovering in or blowing out cash in their attempt to control the money supply. Otherwise it costs $2 for individuals and $5 for families.

The Supreme Court of Canada

Though most Canadians know we have a Queen, few realize there's a small crowd of Lords and Ladies on Wellington Street who exercise great influence on how Canada functions. The nine scarlet monks, or Santas-in-training, make up Canada's highest legal vaudeville stage, and are flatteringly addressed by their former partners and juniors as "My Lord/Lady" or "Your Lordship/Ladyship." Sure, other levels of federal and provincial courts hear the same phrases, but at this level you feel the arguing lawyers really, really mean it. This powerful yet seldom-observed court (though it occasionally serves as a summer replacement for the Commons on the Parliamentary Channel) now has two women – only the second and third appointed in the history of the Court.

The nine scarlet monks, or Santas-in-training, make up Canada's highest legal vaudeville stage, and are flatteringly addressed by their former partners and juniors as "My Lord/Lady" or "Your Lordship/Ladyship."

The Supreme Court existed only as a constitutional clause until 1875, when Parliament finally got around to passing the needed legislation. The Court functioned in obscurity, neglect, and occasional embarrassment until 1949, when it managed to get independence from the Privy Council. And 33 years later the Court took on its most dramatic and important legal and political role when Trudeau's Charter of Rights was sprung on the country. Appeals and challenges to Canadian law based on the Charter have often sent Justice Ministers scurrying to fix or finesse laws decreed rotten by the Court for one reason or another. But sometimes governments have been cowed into non-action, citing the likelihood of the Court striking them down. However, no matter how inconvenient the Charter can be to those governing, it's become a staple cash-crop for legalists. In fact, many Cabinet ministers can hardly wait to get back in private practice and pick a few bales themselves.

All the fun takes place in the striking Ernest Cormier/Mackenzie King–designed building west of Parliament Hill, next to the ugly Archives of Canada, which is done in the depressing Pearson school of architecture. The courtroom in which the Supremes sit is only one of three in the building. The other two are used by judges of the Federal Court of Canada, who also serve as hardy squash and tennis opponents for testosterone-laden Supreme Court justices looking to thrash someone on an international, American, or clay court.

Life on the court is one of hard work, stiff competition, and membership fees.

What I love is hearing vigorous arguments, and then interpreting the law.

Of course, the greatest joy of being the highest court is overturning those irksome calls by umpires just because we can.

Gaining a seat on the Supreme Court carries few requirements: having 10 years of legal practice and being less than 75 years of age are about it. But there's one other, BIG exception: one third of the Court must be from Quebec, with knowledge of Quebec's Civil Code. From that vast pool, the Prime Minister can appoint anyone to the highest bench, without oversight or questioning. Of the nine sitting judges, eight were appointed by Brian Mulroney. The ninth, Antonio Lamer, was elevated by Pierre Trudeau, though Mulroney tapped him to be Chief Justice in 1990.

The feared Red Monks and Monkettes of the Supreme Court in festive native dress.

Chief Justice Lamer is third in the official Table of Precedence, theoretically marching behind the Governor General and the Prime Minister in all parades and ceremonies. As Chief Justice he serves as First-Runner-Up for the Governor General when the latter is away or indisposed. Or deposed, for it's the Chief Justice who fills in during that awkward period when one pair of Their Excellencies are chucked out and the new pair of Their Excellencies have yet to be sworn in (also, ahem, done by the Chief Justice).

The Right Honourable Antonio Lamer sports the dignified, quizzically bemused look of Laurence Olivier in the 1978 film version of Harold Robbins's *The Betsy*. As for a little colour … back in 1968, while practising criminal law (is there any other kind? –ed.), Lamer successfully defended flaming separatist Pierre Bourgault on the charge of inciting the famous St. Jean Baptiste parade riot that provided heroic, myth-making pictures of Pierre Trudeau standing up to the rioters.

The Chief Justice dismisses the growing belief that the Supreme Court is making law rather than interpreting it by saying "We're in the field of pathology. We get the sick laws … We don't get the good and clear laws." Putting that in CBC drama terms, think of *Side Effects* meets *Street Legal*.

The Armed Forces

To most people visiting Ottawa, the Canadian Armed Forces are those brave little bear-skinned extras known as the Governor General's Foot Guards, who chew up the grass in front of the Centre Block. Other than smashing some unsuspecting worms or insects while going through their paces – or themselves during the odd fainting spell – they're relatively harmless, cheery in their scarlet serge, and good for the tourist business. The real soldiers in Ottawa are rarely spotted unless forced to hold a news conference apologizing for some new video. This is unlike the situation in Washington, D.C., where sometimes it seems that half the city is in uniform. The contrast is one of the many blessings of being a middle power.

Another blessing is having a military more concerned with personal promotion

There have been unsettling media spins put upon the perceived distance between me and what's-his-name...the minister fellow.

There is no reason for it. My relationship since returning to CDS has been professional, cordial, and punishingly less than dull.

We have continued fine operations in diverse parts of the world. Though I opposed it, the government had the right to disband the Airborne.

And our widely respected crack pizza delivery corps and videographer section. But poor morale is hardly the problem.

Esprit de corps is. And if I see anyone reading that putrid little magazine, well they sure won't skinny out of a court-martial.

Or maybe at the very least we'll break them down to Brigadier-General.

than with interfering in the civil life of a nation. But budget cuts have reshaped the command structure of our Armed Forces. With about 70,000 "part one" strength members, the Regular Force has dropped to about 95 assorted general-level officers. Notice has been given that by 1998 they'll shed another 25. So, instead of a general for each of the 114 Leopard tanks, there'll be a general for each of our M-109 self-propelled howitzers.

All in all, there are about 16,000 active military officers in Canada. However, the promotion mania in our Armed Forces has reverted to the other ranks, where future frustrated generals and military dictators cool their heels while shining their toe-caps. We've got a military teeming with little corporals – 24,000 of them. Of the very lowest rank, private soldier, there are but 17.

Corporals and generals all have new uniforms, which at least hint at the occupant's branch of service, whether it be by land, air, or sea. Former Liberal Defence Minister Paul Hellyer's Glad-bag green has given way to the bus-driver blue of the Air Force, the seasonal sands and vegetal hues of the Land Force, the deep blues and whites of the Maritime Force, and the brilliant oranges and reds of the Pizza Delivery Force that has grown to supplement a soldier's pay. Their equipment might have once personally been visited by Lester Pearson or John Diefenbaker, but it's said clothes make the man. Not the toys.

The promotion mania in our Armed Forces has reverted to the other ranks, where future frustrated generals and military dictators cool their heels while shining their toe-caps.

The commander-in-chief of the Canadian Armed Forces is the Governor General, and the military is answerable to Parliament through the Minister of National Defence. Giving the minister guidance, planning support, and free tattoo and airshow tickets is the Chief of Defence Staff (CDS). General John de Chastelain – the only general in Canada sporting four maple leaves on his epaulettes – is the once and current Chief, having returned from his position as ambassador in Washington to make way for Jean Chrétien's nephew. He was given the Washington post by a grateful Brian Mulroney, who, through de Chastelain, was able to make war on Saddam Hussein with only some dodgy aircraft, a few aging destroyers armed with weapons borrowed from museums, and some loaves and fishes.

More miracles are needed if the Armed Forces is to overcome a rocky start to the Chrétien era. Soldiers on welfare, a Somalia cover-up, the disbanding of the Airborne Regiment, hazing controversies, Bosnian hostage duty, budget cuts, plummeting morale and aircraft, and ancient equipment have punished a CDS who's already offered his resignation to the Prime Minister and could legally take retirement. But with all his problems, de Chastelain has one that's even bigger – how to keep his slap-headed minister from dressing up in uniform and causing further embarrassment to a reeling Canadian military.

Spooks

With just a simple scanner from Radio Shack, almost anyone in Ottawa has the opportunity to join the ranks of intelligence gatherers. With literally, um, dozens of urgent cellular-phone calls each day capable of producing nothing more than a slight drowsiness or numbness, the capital's radio waves are positively crackling with double-secret government information. Er, like when Diane Marleau wants her limo. When Sergio Marchi wants his limo washed. When Roy MacLaren can't find his other bicycle clip, and someone had better get to Canadian Tire quick for a replacement. Or what some geeky EX1-class civil servant thinks of another geeky EX1-class civil servant's chance for that new position in Vegreville, Alberta. If you kept the receipt, you could probably return the scanner.

Actually picking off cell-phone calls was good enough for Muldoon's government whenever provincial premiers found themselves marooned in Ottawa for endless constitutional arm-twisting. Some premiers learned that the federal government is keen to scavenge, but the public hasn't come to realize this yet.

There are various organizations carrying on intelligence-gathering within the federal government. The RCMP continues to spend about $10 million ferreting out information it believes it needs, though it no longer steams open letters, burns barns, or ushers about cipher clerks sporting bags over their heads. Most of the comic routines were stripped from the RCMP and turned over to a new troupe – the Canadian Security Intelligence Service, or CISSIES. With the suspiciously eager help of foreign intelligence services, CISSIES was set up and launched upon an unsuspecting country and world. Union leaders, Free Trade opponents, journalists, pets,

Hi, I'm Gray Herb, here to tell you about our challenging world of intelligence gathering.

Er...

We gather intelligence and it's challenging. The end.

and children have never been the evil menace they once were, thanks to CISSIES's brilliant newspaper and magazine clipping service and vast array of file folders and classification stamps. CISSIES spends about $200 million a year, and for amusement feuds with the RCMP or resettles and protects CISSIES poster boy Grant Bristow from the dangers of *Toronto Star* reporters. CISSIES don't carry guns, they use their heads. Which often means that the profusion of cuts and bandages on their foreheads gives them away.

CISSIES don't carry guns, they use their heads. Which often means that the profusion of cuts and bandages on their foreheads gives them away.

While the RCMP and CISSIES are answerable to the Solicitor General and some degree of public review, the real intelligence clearing house and sales office is the Privy Council Office. As well as the really important stuff from the Solicitor General, the PCO draws in the goods from the huge, invasive electronic listening post known as the Canadian Security Establishment (CSE), which consumes an unspecified tens of millions of dollars of the Defence Department's budget. This is probably our most dangerous but unknown government creature, and even though the Liberals have promised some sort of monitoring agency for CSE, don't hold your breath. The sweeping abilities and mandate of CSE make it too valuable to be put at risk from an outraged public.

Occasional dollops of interesting stuff also flows into the PCO from an $18-million spook force in Foreign Affairs and an even smaller one in Immigration. And elements of the National Research Council and the Canadian International Development Agency can also be counted as part of our "intelligence community."

The Liberal Party

While the twentieth century didn't exactly belong to Canada, Canada sure as hell belonged to the Liberals. The long decades of power created a comfortable One-Party State, despite occasional sputterings of Western protest and the Diefenbaker and Clark anomalies. The giggle-juice of power flowed freely from Mackenzie King to Louis St. Laurent to Lester Pearson and then Pierre Trudeau, until Trudeau and the gang, eventually realizing the party was definitely over, ducked out in a hurry, leaving the mess and dumpsters full of old empty soldiers for John Turner to clear out. He was caught moving the evidence and bodies into various diplomatic and other patronage positions, and the result was almost a decade of Mulroney and tortured internal Liberal political thumb-sucking and warfare.

When Jean Chrétien emerged victorious at the 1990 leadership convention, with his small throng of wise guys waving Turner's head on a pole, all that had to be done was to wait for the politically dead Muldoonites to drop the writ. Power was certain to be restored – without the bother of ideology or stated policy. And though the kind of ideological spelunking Chrétien and his government have been able to do – moving free of encumbrances in a gleeful dance called "pragmatism" – has an ancient lineage dating back to Mackenzie King, and even Laurier, it wasn't always so.

The original Canadian Liberals emerged in the run-up to Confederation. A loose assembly called the Clear Grits – from a favoured grade of sand Scottish stonemasons liked to use for mortar – was made up of strongly principled, dour Presbyterian and Methodist Upper Canadians. Their leaders were George Brown and Alexander Mackenzie. The cleanliness and purity of the sand was used by one member as an oratorical symbol for the type of man the party wanted – tough and pure. Like most strongly principled nineteenth-century parties, the Clear Grits fell apart, and a new collection of liberal-republican–minded groups came together,

As a true liberal Liberal, fighting the neo-con con, I have banded with other outcasts sharing a vision of a progressive society.

We have concerns about the deficit panic that has infected this government. We firmly believe there are options being ignored.

We are reduced to pinning our hopes on Svend here winning the NDP leadership race.

...and then this potato goop dropped into the hot oil, and believe it or not you had freakin' french fries!

You've obviously mistaken me for someone who gives a damn.

including *les Rouges* from Quebec. Eventually Alexander Mackenzie took the Group, now called Liberals (though they kept the nickname "Grits"), to power in 1874. After losing the next election to the Tories, they replaced Mackenzie with Edward Blake, which merely resulted in the creation of the only Liberal leader to never become Prime Minister. (And people wonder why Liberals think of themselves as divinely ordained to govern Canada!)

Once it was learned that strong, publicly stated ideas and moral inflexibility meant perpetual opposition, it took Blake's anointed successor, Wilfrid Laurier, to fudge things to a degree that helped get Liberals into the Commons' seats nearest the head of the Mace. Laurier's long success in forming the government gave future Liberals the model: keep a workable English–French alliance, soft-sell, and be flexible.

Power is the only thing that motivates a Liberal when you cut through the fashionable political underbrush of the day. It is the true grit that binds them all together.

After World War II, Liberals hit on the three key elements needed to update and animate the Laurier model: money, image, and polling. These elements were fused into the fabled Liberal Machine. Patronage – paid out in contracts or appointments – is the traditional fuel of choice. Through polling, advertising, and fund-raising, a sort of unique royal jelly is force-fed into Liberal leaders to turn them into prime ministers. However, a shortage or shoddy, rotten supply of one or all of this trio of ingredients immediately gets blamed on the leader, so his failure to grow into power becomes his own fault. The only example is John Turner. But it's one not lost on future Liberal players.

Brian Muldoon's one brainstorm was to closely follow the basic Laurier principles, and create a Tory political machine on the Liberal model: Allan Gregg replaced Martin Goldfarb in political-polling legend; fund-raising was put on a shockingly efficient computerized footing (one that Stevie Cameron is still trying to sort through); and image and advertising professionals were easily the equal of Grits, but often had their plans upset or destroyed by an inspired, spontaneously combustible Prime Minister. However, Rome wasn't built in a day, and the gears of the imitation Liberal Party machine crashed and burned in a manner that genuine Liberal parts, tempered by decades of power, have managed to avoid.

REDBOOK

September 1993

Free (You Get What You Pay For)

Drive Them Wild in Polls

The Surprising Places the Public Wants Us to Touch On

TOO LITTLE MONEY?

How to pretend you'll spend anyway

YOUNGER IMAGE

Peter Donolo Shares His Make-Up Tips

ALMOST NOTHING ABOUT THE CONSTITUTION

What Voters Should Never Know about Their Government

EMERGENCY

You Should Have Got It in Writing. Oh. You Did.

September Contents

On our cover:
JEAN CHRÉTIEN/MADAME TUSSAUD

Pg. 96
Who's Tory now, Michael Wilson?

Pg. 84
Could you be accused of Liberalism?

Pg. 22
Man in motion: Paper...Scissors...ROCK! Can the legal superstar slash through the red tape and paper mountain in Ottawa to introduce policies designed to anger diverse interest groups and backbenchers?

Pg. 112
An inch-by-inch guide to Eddie Goldenberg

Contents

Pg. 88 **Protecting Canada's culture is our sacred obligation.**

Figurehead's TelePrompTer

Da key to hour success as a national political party 'as been hour ability to change face, to hadapt, and prevail. Dat will be da key to hour future. Dat is why, himmediately upon my helection as leader of da Liberal Party some t'ree year ago, I set in motion a process to develop a new agenda and a new plan for a new government, which was to be us.

To govern in da 1990s da Liberal Party 'ave to adapt to himmense change in Canada and da world since it left hoffice kicking and screaming in 1984. I hask members of my caucus to stop complaining habout me and to consult wid Canadian and prepare discussion paper on a wide range of hissue. We sponsor Ping-Pong table discussion across Canada on subject such as da heconomy, da henvironment, trade, and foreign policy.

In November 1991 I convene da Aylmer Conference, which brought togedder hexpert from Canada, da United State, Europe, and Japan. I set hout as da purpose of dat conference to challenge conventional wisdom, to get back in power, and try some new policy and happroach dat will give us da balance to be once more da government. Dat conference, like da Kingston Conference before in 1960, mark a turning point for da Liberal Party, except it was not in Kingston, and it was no longer 1960.

In February 1992 a National Liberal Party Convention, bringing togedder t'ousand of Liberal from hacross Canada, pass a series of resolution setting hout hobjective for a new Liberal government when we are once more da government.

T'roughout 1992 and da first half of 1993, hour Platform Committee, co-chair by Paul Martin and Chaviva Hošek, built on da work of 1990 and 1991, which was like dat of 1960 but not in Kingston, and travel hacross Canada, meeting and listening to t'ousand of Canadian. I yam proud dat we took time to reflect, time to consult, and time to listen to Canadian. For at da time, dat what we 'ave plenty of.

Da result is a Liberal plan for Canada firmly hanchor in da sand of time, on da principle dat governing is habout being da government, and dat government must be judged by its heffectiveness in da poll. Dis is our happroach shot, and I yam to try 'ere to make an eagle. Hexcuse me.

September 1993

The Reform Party

The Reform Party of Canada came into existence in 1987. But a bitter split continues to rip apart communities in Alberta and British Columbia about how Reform happened, pitting those who believe in the party's Creation, against those who believe in Evolution.

Creationists see Reform as part of a divine plan set into motion long ago, one that is beyond the understanding of men. This theory is faithfully supported by academics, journalists, Calgary oilmen and others holding to questionable ethics or moral systems.

Creationists see Reform as part of a divine plan set into motion long ago, one that is beyond the understanding of men.

According to their theory, before there was the party, there was the word. And the word could be found in an ancient text published in 1967, written by Ernest and Preston Manning. It was called *Political Realignment: A Challenge to Thoughtful Canadians*, and it warned that the growing betrayal of conservatives demanded that a new coalition party be cobbled together from the old parties. If that didn't happen, they said, Canada would then see the creation of an entirely new party by aroused and concerned small-c conservatives. Ernest Manning, Social Credit Premier of Alberta from 1943 to 1968 – and the heir of Bible Bill Aberhart's colourful mantle and radio show, which marked one as anointed back then – schooled his son Preston well in the mysteries. As no coalition formed, both Mannings waited for the inevitable.

After a few false starts, western rage against the Mulroney Tories provided all the ingredients for the Big Bang, which came with Reform's 1987 founding assembly in Vancouver. Preston Manning, following the script of *Political Realignment* and Mulroney's spoor, turned Western alienation into the new party of the right, and marched into Ottawa with 52 seats in the last election.

(Scientific Creationists believe much the same thing, but claim that Calgary oilmen, with extra cash, time, and resentment on their hands, wanted to form a new political party, and were casting about for a leader, when someone mentioned that Ernest Manning's son was probably free. Which, as it turns out, he was.)

Those who believe in Evolution – the rank and file – are outside the loop of Reform's power centre in Calgary. Reform's existence to them is the result of natural selection over many decades, during which beasts that once roamed the west in large herds, such as the Co-operative Commonwealth Federation, the Progressives, and Social Credit, eventually refined their opposable thumbs and grassroots brain into today's party members. Evolutionists believe that process and populism, not a divine spark or hand, brought the party into being.

This bitter division of beliefs within Reform plagues the party. Leader Preston Manning, his loyal band of flunkies at the party controls, and Reform caucus members themselves often move from one camp to another in times of trial – especially when there are likely to be microphones around. The party is the grass roots. The party is the leader. The leader follows the grass roots. The grass roots follows the leader. Reform policy is made by the leader's loyalists in Calgary. Reform policy is made by the caucus listening to their constituents. No wonder Reformers have a slight glaze to their eyes. Those who think about it are stuck trying to rationalize two incompatible assets – a strong, autocratic leader and populism. Their heads hurt.

Rolling into Ottawa with 51 of 86 seats in Western Canada, and only one seat east of Manitoba, Reformers were going to clean up Parliament. After all, they were now the true Loyal Opposition because the Bloc were avowed separatists. So caucus members didn't shadow issues or ministers, they floated. Preston Manning wasn't in the opposition front bench, he was just "one of the folk" in the back rows. What's more, Reformers didn't accept full salaries – they cut them by 10% (even if that meant getting 6% back in tax receipts). And Preston didn't take some of his perks. However, when the media learned of party expense accounts for Preston and his wife, Sandra ($31,000 and $12,000, no receipts required), combined with some of the grumbling from caucus about the voluntary pay cuts, Reform looked dangerously close to being another party corrupted by Ottawa. Also cutting into their support was that they yammered about Quebec and the constitution just like everyone else. Turning Reform benches into a command post for a non-existent tax revolt, or running rather pointless interactive television shows, didn't help much either. Continuing bad media reviews,

If you want to know what I think of same-sex benefits, well, to be honest, I'm all for them.

Why should anyone be penalized for choosing a lifestyle that may be entirely a genetic thing anyway?

There's a security issue here. People need to feel that, no matter what happens in their lives, there are things they can depend on. Like clockwork. Saturday mornings at 9:30.

You see, Sandra and I have been having the same sex for decades now, and if that qualifies us for some sort of tax break or compensation, then we're there.

tumbling poll numbers, and a non-existent national profile brought swift changes only months after arriving in Ottawa. As a result, Manning slipped down to the front bench. A caucus revolt led to a form of shadow cabinet, and when consultants were hired, Reform performances during Oral Questions and their chances of getting clipped during scrums improved. They were no longer unable or unwilling to go whining and snivelling and yelping after weak ministers and proto-scandals. Reform was fitting in.

To those back in the ridings, it looked like their honourable members were going native. But the transformation worked just fine.

Despite the party's teething pains and just plain goofy calls, the biggest threat to Reform, outside of its internal paradox and structural fragility, is that now the Liberal Party – as it did to the CCF and NDP decades ago – is poaching policy. Law and order. Tougher sentencing of criminals. Tough immigration restrictions. Decentralization. And the overriding fiscal panic and sudden budget cuts to fight the deficit. They weren't in the Red Book. But it's all been in the Blue Book for years.

And again this opens yet another rift in Reform. Preston and the gentle gloss he puts on a tough, right-wing party are calculated designs to gain power in the next election. But hard-line conservatives in the party, and those flocking around it, are happy enough to stay true to the cause, linger in opposition, avoid compromise, and force the changes they want on a less scrupulous, but power-thirsty party.

If you want to observe the populist phenomenon up close, here's how to blend in

Don't insult the leader. Don't insult the grass roots. Reformers try not to dwell on the problems of trying to follow both. When either comes up, be gentle and positive. Don't force your contact to do injury trying to resolve the unresolvable. No German jokes.

Wear clothes that will make the contact comfortable. If your suit cost more than large livestock, leave it at home or in the hotel room. No one, outside of Preston, wears clothes like that. Both Harpers (see below) – and some of the Germans – wear single-breasted suits of dark blue. A European double-breasted suit such as worn by the leader, in any colour but Bloc standard-issue grey, may be worn when meeting Preston or senior critics. Blazer and grey flannel trousers are also fine, unless the blazer is too finely tailored or new, or bears a crest. Shiny suits and furs have been seen on Herb Grubel. Enough said. Be prepared for casual attire during bouts of parliamentary committee work, with western-tailored shirts, jackets, ties, and boots all possible. Do not attempt wearing these yourself, unless you habitually do. You'll merely offend your contact and look silly. Sweaters are not advisable, as they scream academic humanism, aggressive informality, or Easterner. Power ties and power tie-knots are definitely to be avoided. A four-in-hand knot is the only one recommended. Do not wear a bow-tie unless you are dining formally (unlikely) or are a journalist.

52 Strong, But We Need to GROW!

"Give me the tools, and I'll finish the job!"

Help bring Reform and Reformers to Ottawa.

NOW!

Paid for by the
Wild Rose of Taxes Committee,
Calgary, Alberta

REFORM PARTY OF CANADA

Women are strongly advised to study the wardrobes of Diane Ablonczy, Val Meredith and Margaret Bridgman. If you can't recall anything of note about these MPs, then you've learned all you need to. Unassuming. Bland. Inoffensive. Avoid Jan Brown ensembles, unless you have the hair for it, and the array of vests utilized by Deborah Grey, unless you have the build to pull it off.

Reform Movers, Shakers, and Other Holy Rollers

Ernest Charles Manning: Father to the son. A disciple of Alberta Social Credit premier Bible Bill Aberhart, the elder Manning followed Aberhart in the Social Credit premiership and radio ministry, serving from 1943 to 1968. Passing on his politics, faith, speaking manner, and bold charisma to Preston, the two worked so closely together for so long that many can't tell where one ends and the other begins.

Ernest Preston Manning: Son to the father. He's the whole party franchise, and this is resented by a party right wing that questions the leader's orthodoxy. Strange among Canadian leaders in that he actually reads books: the problem is more what he retains from them. Histories of the American Civil War, Prairie populism and protest movements, and stolid overviews are always good gifts, and have strongly flavoured his views of Quebec and Reform Party administration. An adherent of the systems-analysis school of problem-solving, he advocates managed conflict resolution but hates any sort of confrontation, preferring to cut it off and toss it out. By all accounts he's nice to children, dogs, and visiting Africans. But Preston has developed a tolerance for hypocrisy, likely due to his long-standing ability to divorce his intense private morality from his less rigorous public threshold.

Sandra Manning: Wife to the son. Mother of his five children. She's also an outspoken adviser with unequalled access to the leader, unafraid to provide counsel on political strategy, policy, staffing, and wardrobe. She has designed a system to allow Preston to dress himself on the road without embarrassment, and has advised Reform women on how to pare down clothing expenses. Sandra loomed large on election night, but has failed to increase her presence or role, having suffered a few tough passes with the media. Her husband had her parachuted into a Reform Party position that drew a $12,000 receipt-free expense allowance, thereby waking his own $31,000 sleeping dog.

Reform Party Executive Council: Now at 24 elected members and based in Calgary, it has been the key warehouse for Manning-approved loyalists, allowing the leader to exercise his administrative will over the Reform Party. Some key members of Reform's caucus are former members of the council. Since the election, fire-fights between caucus and Calgary over policy and direction have flared up.

Party Policy Committee: The major tool used by Manning to keep embarrassing, unsound, or crazy riding association resolutions from entering Reform policy books. Its members handpicked by Manning, and answerable to Manning, it has often been used to show the leader as a control freak.

Diane Ablonczy: The Reform Party's first chair, a former executive assistant to the leader, and one of the clique around Manning that offended some Reformers and led to charges of elitism. Her sister, Danita Onyebuchi, has served as her stunt double in the party structure. Ablonczy, now in the Commons, serves wherever Preston tells her to, without question or discouraging word.

Ray Speaker: A chum of Preston's at the University of Alberta who is a former Social Credit MLA and an Alberta Tory minister. Ray bolted from Don Getty to the new party a few years ago. Sensitive tasks such as overseeing the creation of a code of conduct for the caucus have fallen to him. In 1994 he led the caucus revolt that demanded traditional shadow responsibilities. Speaker splits duties as Finance critic with Herb Grubel, and is one to watch.

Deborah Grey: Elected as the first Reform MP in 1989, the former Beaver River schoolteacher was selected for her evangelical beliefs and charm. Grey now sits to Manning's right in the front row, and holds the postion of caucus chair. Er, that's it.

Stephen Harper: The 35-year-old Harper was hailed by the *Globe and Mail* as one of the most important neo-conservatives in Canada. A former Tory, Harper defeated his former boss, MP James Hawkes, in the last election. Preston has become accustomed to watching his back. Harper had difficulties with Manning when the ideologically impure Rick Anderson was brought in as campaign director in 1993. And he displeased Manning with his questioning of the leader's secret expense account.

You guys reporting on my $31,000 slush – I mean expense – allowance have exaggerated this thing. It's not as if it's in U.S. dollars or anything.

Most Reformers are willing to make sacrifices to help the nation's finances. Except me. It's my Party, and I'll buy suits if I want to.

Y'know, looking around at you guys, you wouldn't want me to go out dressed that badly, would you?

And actually the $31,000 doesn't go far. Nine or ten suits, a few buck white loafers, and a few good pointy boots. Thank God for Sandra's allowance, or our kids'd starve.

As one of the party's founders, Harper was Reform's Chief Policy Officer and a key adviser before finally gaining a seat in 1993 (he was defeated in 1988). Both Harper and Manning are expert at shepherding Reform assemblies through contentious debates and resolutions, securing the desired results without the flock noticing the manipulation. Harper is touted as the heir to Manning; his bilingualism and party stature have earned him the post of National Unity–Constitutional Affairs critic, and the shadowing of Marcel Massé on Intergovernmental Affairs.

Ed Harper: The sole Reform MP elected east of Manitoba, the former tire salesman and alderman from Barrie, Ontario, also holds the only non-Liberal seat in Ontario. This status gives him some heft among caucus and the media. He serves as Stephen Harper's helpmate with the Constitution.

Elwin Hermanson: Reform House Leader and a former, multiple-term member of the party's Executive Council, which means he is thoroughly trusted by Manning to share views and comprehend the leader's wishes.

Rick Anderson: Reform campaign director for the 1993 election (and Manning's acting chief of staff until replaced by Stephen Greene), the blond, bearded spin doctor is an executive vice-president with the infamous Hill & Knowlton public-affairs agency. Manning's engagement of Anderson, formerly a Liberal, employed by John Turner, upset Reform ideological hardliners like Stephen Harper. Hill & Knowlton can and has sold, rehabilitated, or secured everything under the sun. It brings to mind Mordecai Richler's statement: "[Manning is] a menacingly sweet man. I think, if fascism ever came to this country, the fascists would be wearing Boy Scout uniforms." Be prepared.

Don't insult the leader. Don't insult the grass roots. Reformers try not to dwell on the problems of trying to follow both.

Tom Flannagan: A former policy adviser to Manning, Flannagan was fired/resigned in 1993 after fighting with the leader over Rick Anderson. An American, Flannagan is a professor at the University of Calgary, and has since been sniping at Manning and the party, claiming the leader is not ideologically pure in his conservatism. Flannagan is a frequent media expert on Reform, and his recent book on Manning and the party continues to bemoan Manning's conservative betrayal. A man to watch, especially if the battle between Manning and Stephen Harper renews.

Cliff Fryers: A powerful Calgary lawyer and former party chairman who is still a respected Reform force. One of Manning's toughest loyalists, he voluntarily took himself out of the spotlight but still lurks.

Ron Wood: Longtime, deeply trusted Preston Manning press secretary until ill health forced him to pull back from the daily grind. Like Fryers, he was invaluable in getting Reform through the early years and into the House.

REFORM
PARTY OF CANADA

Minister: Ernest P. Manning
Pianist: Sandra Manning

Annual Ecumenical Open Invitational Service

APPROACHING POWER THROUGH WORSHIP

Piano Prelude
Opening Words and Welcome

Hymn: "Onward! Preston Soldiers", #55

LISTENING AND REFLECTING ON THE SCRIPTURES 1
Scriptures from the Old Canada: Exodus 15:1–12

Time with the Younger Reformers

Hymn: "This Little Reform Light of Mine," Children's Blue Book, #3

Silent Reflection
Grass-roots Offering and Dedication

Reform Party Creed
I vainly affirm the need to establish a Triple-E Senate in the Parliament of Canada – that is to say, a Senate that is Elected by the people, with Equal representation from each Province, and that is fully Effective in safeguarding regional interests. I affirm that political parties should be guided by stated values and principles that are shared by their members as selected by the Leader and rooted in the political beliefs of Canadians as divined by the Leader. I believe in dynamic and constructive change – in a renewal of the "reform tradition" of Canadian politics, subject to approval by the Leader.

I believe in the Leader, the Reform Party, the Executive Council, the subservience of the elected body in Ottawa, and the right of recall. Yee Haw!

LISTENING AND REFLECTING ON THE SCRIPTURES 2
Scriptures from the Old Canada: Exodus 24:1–11

Closing Words
Piano Postlude
Race for the Door

Exodus

Being the Second Book of Preston

Chapter 15

Then sang Pre'-ston and the children of Re'-form this song unto the Leader, and spake, saying I will sing unto the Leader, for he hath triumphed gloriously: the ministers and their drivers hath he thrown into the sea.
2. Pre'-ston is my strength and song, and he is become my salvation: he is my Leader, and I will prepare him a habitation allowance, and one for clothing; his father was Er'-nest, and I will exalt him.
3. The Leader is a man of war: Pre'-ston is his name.
4. Mul'-ro-ney's chariots and his host hath he cast into the sea: his chosen ministers also are drowned in the Peace River.
5. The media have uncovered them; they sank into the bottom of the balloting as a stone.
6. Thy right, O Leader, is become glorious in power: thy right, O Leader, hath dashed off great policy. Thy right hand, O Leader, was Ste'-phen Har'-per, but he pisseth thee off. Thy left offend thee too, and it has been cut in pieces, unto nine seats.
7. And in the greatness of thine excellency thou has overthrown them that rose up in the House against thee: thou sentest forth thy eastern rallies, which undercuttest their number.
8. And with the blast of thy nostrils the voters were gathered together; they stood up upright in a heap, and not upon their knuckles.
9. The enemy said, I will pursue, I will overtake, I am the re-elect; my lust shall be satisfied upon them; I will draw my six gun, my momentum shall destroy them.
10. Thou didst blow with thy wind the ballots that covered them: they sank as their early lead in the polls evaporated.
11. The Leader shall reign for ever and ever.
12. For the stalking horse of Mul'-ron-ey went in with her chariots and with her horsemen unto the voters, and the Leader brought again the voters of Al-ber'-tah upon them; but the children of Re'-form went on dry-riding upon the crest of the wave.

Chapter 24

And when the people saw that Pre'-ston delayed to come up to the Hill, the people gathered themselves together unto Cliff, and said unto him, Up, make us good suits, which shall go before us; for as for this Pre'-ston, the man that brought us up out of the land of Al'-ber'-tah, we wot not what is become of him.
2. And Cliff said unto them, Break off the golden earrings, which are in the ears of your wives, of your sons, and of your daughters, and bring them unto me, and taketh a partial tax deduction.
3. And all the people broke off the golden earrings which were in their ears, and brought them unto Cliff, and tooketh a partial tax deduction.
4. And he received them at their hand, and fashioned it with a lawyer's pen, after he had made it an expense account: and they said, This be for the good suits, O Re'-form-ers, which brought thee up out of the land of Al'-ber'-tah.
5. And when Cliff saw it, he built a smaller one before it for the wife called San'-dra, and Cliff made a memo to the Executive Council proclaiming the deed as done and of limited circulation, and said, Tomorrow is a feast to the good suits, and receipts are needeth not, for in him we trust.
6. And they rose up early on the morrow, and offered questions and wondered why no receipts were offered, and no apologies, and the people sat down to wonder if all was as it was cracked up to be.
7. And the Er'-nest said unto Pre'-ston, go, get thee down; for thy people, which thou broughtest out of the land of Al-ber'-tah have corrupted themselves and talketh to the media.
8 They have turned aside quickly out of the way which I commanded them: they have made them a collection of good suits, and have worshipped it, and have sacrificed thereunto, and are sorely pissed for the receipts offered not by that which have brought thee out of Al-ber'-tah.
10. And the Er'-nest said unto Pre'-ston, I have seen this people, and, behold it is a rednecked people:
11. Now therefore let me alone, and go down among Re'-form and try to explain away this one for thou surely are on thy own, and must cover thy nakedness. Or hypocrisy. I forgeteth which.

55. Onward! Preston Soldiers

ONWARD! Preston soldiers,
Marching at the fore,
No one knows but Manning
What we have in store.
He's the one true leader
Stalling in the poll
Forward into battle,
Hope the rallies grow.

Onward! Preston soldiers,
Off to slay the Whore.
With the Son of Ernest
Whining on some more.

2 As the Speaker riseth,
Chrétien's host doth flee;
On then Preston soldiers.
On to the TV!
Th' Hill's foundations quiver
At the din we raise;
Brothers, lift your voices,
Loud your questions raise.

3 Like a mighty army
Moves the proud Reform;
Brothers, we are treading
Troopers of the Storm.
We are not divided,
All one party he,
One in hope, in doctrine,
He alone is he.

4 Towns and homes do perish,
People cannot buy
But the Reform Party
Knows the reason why;
Socialists can never
Save us from the flames;
Lack of family values,
Chief among the blames.

5 Onward, then Reformers
Join our grass-roots mob;
Send us with your ballots
If you have a job.
Glory, suits, and honour
Unto Ernest's son!
End these countless rallies
Myron get your gun!

Children's Hymn

3. This Little Reform Light of Mine

This little Reform light of mine,
I'm gonna let it shine
This little Reform light of mine
I'm gonna let it shine
This little Reform light of mine
I'm gonna let it shine
Let it shine, all the time, let it shine.

Lights always draw a bug or two
I'm gonna let it shine
Lights always draw a bug or two
I'm gonna let it shine
Lights always draw a bug or two
I'm gonna let it shine
All the time, let it shine, let it shine.

We'll squash the bugs, and carry on
I'm gonna let it shine
We'll squash the bugs, and carry on
I'm gonna let it shine
We'll squash the bugs, and carry on
I'm gonna let it shine
Let it shine, let it shine, let it shine.

The flames of hell await for you
We're gonna let them shine
The flames of hell await for you
We're gonna let them shine
The flames of hell await for you
We're gonna let them shine
Let it shine, let it shine, all the time.

Reform Shadow Cabinet

der Leiter **Preston Manning**
Hauptbefehisleiter Economik **Stephen Harper**
Gauleiter Hauptbefehisleiter Economik **Herb Grubel**
Hauptbefehisleiter Gemeinschaft **Stephen Harper**
Gauleiter Hauptbefehisleiter Gemeinschaft **Ed Harper**
Oberbefehisleiter der Fooden **Elwin Hermanson**
Gauleiter Oberbefehisleiter der Fooden **Allan Kerpan**
Gauleiter Oberbefehisleiter der Fooden **Cliff Breitkreuz**
Gauleiter Oberbefehisleiter der Fooden **Jake Hoeppner**
Hauptdienstleiter der Justice **Jack Ramsay**
Gauleiter Hauptdienstleiter der Justice **Diane Ablonczy**
Helfer der Justice **Myron Thompson**
Oberdienstleiter Whippen **Bob Ringma**
Gauleiter Oberdienstleiter Whippen **Jack Frazer**
Oberdienstleiter Ostandervolkenimmigranten und Kanadalandenvolke **Val Meredith**
Rottenführer Ostandervolkenimmigranten und Kanadalandenvolke **Jay Hill**
Hauptbereichsleiter Reichstagleiter **Ray Speaker**
Gauleiter Hauptbereichsleiter Reichstagleiter **Ken Epp**
Hauptabschnittsleiter der Turbot und Flattfischen **Mike Scott**
Oberabschnittsleiter Spooken und Mountie **Art Hanger**
Gauleiter Oberabschnittsleiter Spooken und Mountie **Garry Breitkreuz**
Ortsgruppenleiter Kulturen Kanada Infobahn und Spicer **Monte Solberg**
Gauleiter Ortsgruppenleiter Kulturen Kanada Infobahn und Spicer **Hugh Hanrahan**
Obergemeinschaftsleiter der Reichswehr **Jim Hart**
Gauleiter Obergemeinschaftsleiter der Reichswehr **Jack Frazer**
Obergemeinschaftsleiter der Kustomvolke **Jim Silye**
Obergemeinschaftsleiter der Statenmonie und Regionoperationen und Uberchambervolke **Jim Abbott**
Blockleiter Autobahn Docken und Bonspeil Structuren und Kontract Werkunpublik **Randy White**
Gauleiter Blockleiter Autobahn Docken und Bonspiel Structuren und Kontract Werkunpublik **Bill Gilmour**
Rottenführer Autobahn Docken und Bonspiel Structuren und Kontract Werkunpublik **Dick Harris**
Haupteinsatzleiter Publikservizkaputten **Ian McClelland**
Befehisleiter Humansch Resoursgerspaten Werkfaren und Frauvolke **Jan Brown**
Gauleiter Befehisleiter Humansch Resoursgerspaten Werkfaren und Frauvolke **Dale Johnston**
Oberarbeitsleiter Humansch Resoursgerspaten Werkfaren und Frauvolke **Daphne Jennings**
Hauptbereitschaftsleiter **Deborah Grey**
Oberbereitschaftsleiter Affairen Externerverld und Aiden Schwartzenvolk **Bob Mills**
Gauleiter Oberbereitschaftsleiter Affairen Externerverld und Aiden Schwartzenvolk **Lee Morrison**
Bereitschaftsleiter Economiklebensraum **Werner Schmidt**
Gauleiter Bereitschaftsleiter Economiklebensraum **Phillip Mayfield**
Hauptarbeitsleiter Boarden der Treazur und Soundträcken **John Williams**
Oberarbeitsleiter Druggen und Kleinhealten **Grant Hill**
Gauleiter Oberarbeitsleiter Druggen und Kleinhealten **Sharon Hayes**
Oberarbeitsleiter Realpolitik der Indienvolken **John Duncan**
Gauleiter Oberarbeitsleiter Realpolitik der Indienvolken **Margaret Bridgman**
Oberarbeitsleiter Environmenten **Paul E. Forseth**
Gauleiter Oberarbeitsleiter Environmenten **Keith Martin**
Oberhelfer Transporten **Jim Gouk**
Helfer der Transporten **John Cummins**
Oberhelfer Petrol und Fartgassen **Chuck Strahl**
Helfer der Petrol und Fartgassen **Dave Chatters**
Helfer der Lumberen Angriff **Darell Stinson**
Oberhelfer der Economik Freikorps **Charlie Penson**
Helfer der Economik Freikorps **Leon Benoit**

The Bloc Québécois

The Bloc Québécois was formed from the ashes of Lucien Bouchard's Cabinet career when Bouchard's friendship with Martin Brian Mulroney flamed out over the failure of the Meech Lake agreement. Like Reform, the Bloc is the political equivalent of forest mushrooms, feeding and growing off the decaying dead wood of Muldoon-era Tories.

Though there are at present 53 members of the Bloc sitting in the House of Commons, and the party numbly walks through the role of Her Majesty's Loyal Opposition, there is only one seat that matters – seat number 159, assigned to Lucien Bouchard. Empty for months as Bouchard, like a newt or salamander, tried to grow a new sovereigntist leg to stand on, his Commons desk served as a handy receptacle for floral tributes by Reform's coon skin-capped siren, Jan Brown. Bouchard returned early in 1995, thanking Brown but

There are things that cannot be understood by those who have never made an effort to understand us.

We have been most patient. We have demonstrated the patience of saints. And even saints need a patron to gather around.

When I founded the Bloc, rising from the ashes in our mouths, it was natural for us to remove the bad taste at a St. Hubert.

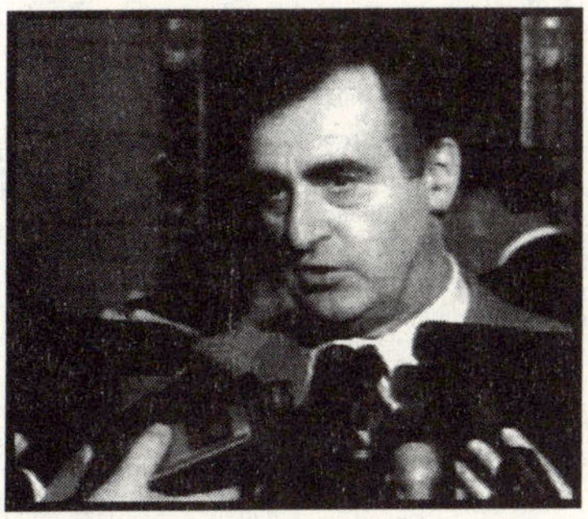

And so we have, and we adopted that gentle, sustaining, winged saint as one of our own...

to help and to guide us in our successful attempt to get finally once and for all separ...

...er...sovereignty-association, building the new supra-national cooperation between Canada and Quebec the polls show we can win with.

still shy one leg himself. To compensate, he produced the perfect Referendum prosthesis to keep Parizeau and the PQ from tumbling to defeat and humiliation. *Virage*. A change of direction. Instead of a simple question on the independence of Quebec, the PQ and the Bloc agreed to do and say anything to get a Yes vote that may later be twisted and finessed and inflated into their own country.

As a result, the Bloc is committed to immediate sovereignty, possible association, er, and whatever Lucien Bouchard says it is. From Ottawa, Bouchard has made half-hearted attempts to harass the federal government, but enjoys far greater success in embarrassing and annoying the One True Government of Quebecers, at present in the hands of PQ Premier Jacques Parizeau. Bouchard and Parizeau two-step with the grace and paranoid, staccato fervour that conjures up images of Ahab and his Great White Whale. Both creatures, fearful of their backs at this critical moment in their plans, realize the best mutual protection is to keep their bellies together.

The remainder of this page has been deleted by the Publishers' Council pending outcome of an unnamed lawsuit in Quebec.

The New Democratic Party

Better known as the New Demographics Party, its new numbers are pretty depressing. The NDP's record support in the polls from 1985 to 1993 – well, the non-election years anyway – gave rise to the belief that the new demographics would indeed turn out to be favourable, and a swell of public adulation would soon fill the benches in the Commons with fields of corduroy, sensible shoes, and tweed sport coats. But two avoidable disasters called Audrey McLaughlin and Bob Rae effectively flat-lined NDP support, ensuring truly piss-poor new demographics, which in turn would unleash a punishing series of "Whither the Left" symposia and the dullest federal leadership campaign since, well, the one that selected Audrey. From a respectable 41 seats, the NDP showed up for the 35th Parliament with only 8 persons, and failed to rate official-party status. Not only that, Audrey McLaughlin lost her Commons' perks and her $29,500 leadership bonus. Whoever succeeds her on October 12 won't get it either.

Which raises this question: who would want to inherit the party? The NDP, flux-soldered and binder-twined together from the agrarian Co-operative Commonwealth Federation and organized labour in 1961, never really lived up to its promise. It certainly never terrified the Liberals into creating new policies, as they did when the CCF was around. And the union leaders were never able to deliver their members' votes. Instead, the party hobbled along functionally but without grace, respectable compared with Social Credit, but harmless to those in power.

Sure, they took provincial capitals, and some NDP orators like Tommy Douglas, or even David Lewis, could raise the temperature a bit on certain issues, recreating the CCF's "conscience of the nation" role. But Eaton's certainly didn't foresee the need to pass out the baseball bats as it did during the Winnipeg General Strike. Nor did anyone else who controlled the means of production or wealth.

The gradual change in the NDP during Ed Broadbent's 14 years as leader left the party without strongly articulated or widely held principles. Instead, it became a buffet table of single-issue interest groups, a left-wing equivalent of Joe Clark's Community of Communities, headed by a leader vastly more popular than his party through longevity and comparison with John Turner and Brian Mulroney.

The lack of unity – or a strong, shared platform – naturally led to Audrey McLaughlin, who won mainly on the momentum of "Well, why not a woman, even if she is a rookie MP with the speaking style of drying bread and an unarticulated vision." The party's central Canadian elite (read: Lewis clan) pumped Audrey as a pristine "empty bottle" that could be filled with vital economic and social ideas. In the end, all the NDP got was, er, an empty bottle – a nice, well-mannered one, mind you, but empty. (The same Lewis clan is supporting former Nova Scotia NDP leader Alexa McDonough as Audrey's replacement. Hasn't the party learned anything about the judgment of these people?)

The NDP's failure to provide strong alternatives to the two major political parties was most evident during the Meech and Charlottetown fandangoes. The NDP leadership, in solidly throwing its support behind both deals, left the majority of Canadians who happened to oppose the constitutional monsters without a voice in Parliament. The frustration meant a lot of people were looking for someone – anyone – who opposed the deals, and they found such a spokesman in Preston Manna.

As a result, the national NDP appeared to be a party just like the rest, working all too easily with the others to stifle dissent. The dramatic U-turns and missteps by the Ontario and British Columbia provincial parties sealed the impression of a party without bottom, direction, or ability.

How leadership candidate Svend Robinson, who's spent most of his apparently inexhaustible 15 minutes of fame fighting for the rights of trees to live and people to die when not staging foreign photo-ops, behaving impolitely, or denouncing Petro-Canada executives as CIA agents, will change this is unclear. Robinson may have done some admirable work championing human rights, but there's already an Amnesty International. Media stunts won't change the position of the NDP, which at present is huddled in a dispirited lump near the curtains in the far corner of the Commons. Neither will the non entities or petty drug-store thieves filling the roles of leadership also-rans.

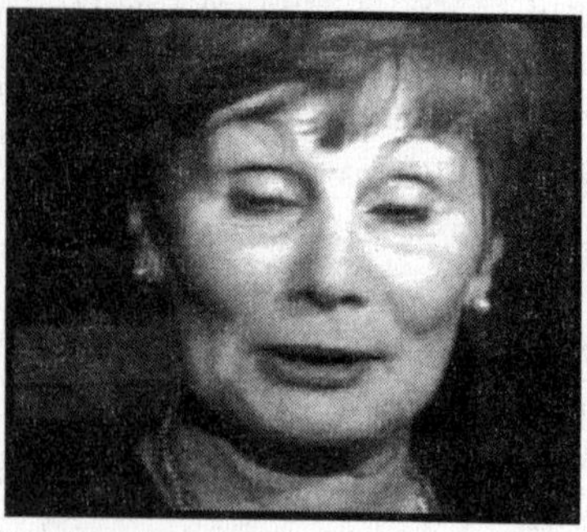

It's time. TIme for that well-pensioned ice flow called "elder statespersonhood."

I have no regrets.

My party might, but it's not around to talk about it, is it?

Louis St. Laurent once dismissed the NDP as "Liberals in a hurry." He was right. It's rushing towards Liberal "pragmatism" – or, as it's popularly known, "weaseling." But the Liberals have decades of practice at that kind of thing, vast piles of loot, and the human talent to pull it off. The NDP doesn't and never will. If the party doesn't come up with more than a few political odds and ends it fervently believes in, it will probably give lemmings a run for their money in the metaphor – or mixed metaphor – department.

The Progressive Conservative Party

Alas, it is the saddest of fates for the party that built (surely bilked? –ed.) this country. From the days when the Tories of John A. Macdonald were in the pockets of our great rail barons, to over a century later, when the Muldoonites finally got around to burying much of the steel spoor, our Tories have occasionally governed Canada when the Grits needed a vacation.

When Tory backroom wise guys chased out Kim Campbell from the leadership in December 1993, with raspy threats that they'd force a money drought if she hung about, Jean Charest finally got what he wanted the previous June – the leadership of the Progressive Conservative Party. The new leader and the led (former Saint John mayor Elsie Wayne) shuffled around the Commons, no longer a recognized party, and not even seated next to each other for comfort. Eventually the seating arrangement changed, but the caucus size won't for years. Avril Kim Campbell, the first Canadian woman to be Prime Minister, did secure another bittersweet first for the PCs – absolute gender equality for the party in the Commons.

But perhaps everybody's being too hard on Campbell. No one the Tories might have hoisted as a banner of change and renewal could have hidden the mark of the Beast – the indelible tattoo of Brian Mulroney they all have on their foreheads. It's going to take a lot of expensive laser surgery and time before Tories can get that one to fade. The Muldoon legacy, and the defection of the part's bitching-but-Blue western base to Reform, threatens the worst. If Reform doesn't collapse in a heap of confused dissent, the Tories will go the way of the British Liberal Party. Or Canada's NDP. Or the Tories, which have already merged once before with a western populist party, will have to do so again.

To avoid that, Charest, a pudgy, rumpled professional politician, spends more time outside the Commons than in it. Which is wise. After a windy reply to the government's first throne speech, Charest

No, I am not worried. We still have the support of hundreds of thousands of Canadians. We're rebuilding.

We're getting our finances in order. We're overtaking Reform at the bottom of the polls. We're redoing policy.

All right, who said "squishie"?

was ridiculed by a Grit back-bencher as "the leader of nothing." It would only have got worse. Better for him to invest time outside the Commons. After all, the Tories had a respectable popular vote in the last election, and still have $3.5 million in trust, control of the Senate, and a growing provincial power-base. But Charest also has to win back Reform converts, fight off the growing threat of Ralph Klein (spotted in June 1995, tearing around the Middle East practising foreign policy), and watch as dweebs like neo-writer David Frum try to reinflate the party with the searing winds of neo-conservatism, designed to make Tories merely young urban Reformers with better suits, self-directed RRSPs, and private health insurance. This infusion of young, cold-blooded hot blood could be attractive, but it's the older Red Tories who know the ropes, phone numbers, and bank accounts that can get – and keep – a party toe to toe with enough treasure and organization to rival the Grits. These fault lines ensure Charest and the Tories will keep the pundits and academics busy up to, and after, the next election.

He haunts us still.
(shurley you mean "creeps us out," not "haunts" – ed.)

In the meantime the nation's revenge is sweet. Most Canadian ears still ring with Mulroney's swaggering bravado about taking two back-to-back majorities and leaving a party poised for a brilliant, long-lived future in power, so watching (when they manage to get a camera pointed their way) the pathetic Pushme-Pullyou routine of the two-person Tory caucus takes the sting out of the Liberals happily using the same Tory economic on-board computer while gleefully shredding copies of their beloved Red Book for gerbil beds.

All of this has to steam Charest, as he scrambles to come up with a platform the Liberals aren't standing and dancing on, and Reformers aren't blasting away at. Even worse, the transformation of True Grits to Blue Grits means that Muldoon will continue to gloat for years to come, whenever given the chance, about how the Tories obviously were doing the right thing, and the Liberals knew it all along. Yeeeesh.

Independent Members of Parliament

Outside of the recognizable parties in the House of Commons, and the ravaged corpses of the semi-official NDP and Tories, there are the Independents, or parties of one. Traditionally, Indies either are rare strikes of political lightning, usually one-termers, who then fall to more established parties at the next general election, or are in a sort of midterm political detox for scandal-laden or rebellious government backbenchers. During the last days of the Muldoonites, a handful of nervous backbenchers were cast out. One, David Kilgour, made the jump to the Liberal Party, and is now Deputy Speaker of the Commons. Of course Liberalism was in his blood. Kilgour's sister is Geills Turner, John's steely-hearted wife.

> **Indies either are rare strikes of political lightning, usually one-termers, who then fall to more established parties at the next general election, or are in a sort of midterm political detox for scandal-laden or rebellious government backbenchers.**

The election of 1993 coughed up one independent – Gilles Bernier of Beauce. Bernier was first elected to the Commons in 1984, and re-elected in 1988. But back then he was a Tory. A broadcaster, hotel-keeper, restaurateur, and Muldoonite facing charges of fraud and breach of trust (eventually acquitted in June 1994), Gilles had his nomination papers filed in the circular bin by former Conservative prime minister Kim Campbell. Her refusal to sign them forced him to run as an Indie, which he did, pulling in 40% of the riding vote.

After the election, Bernier of Beauce was actively, but unsuccessfully, courted by Reform, which has been constantly sniffing about for the two MPs that may give them Official Opposition status (Hello Nelson, Elsie!). Bernier says he owes it to his constituents to remain an Independent, since that was how he ran. While he previously served on Commons' committees during the Tory government, he now wallows in obscurity and emptiness because Indies and the unrecognized parties have no role in House committees. They also have little chance of being recognized during Oral Questions. Luckily, Bernier is already guaranteed a pension, which is something most Independents are rarely around long enough to collect.

The other Indie is the nationally famous Jag Bhaduria. The rubber-haired MP for Markham-Whitchurch-Stouffville was thrown up on the beach, mouth flapping indignantly, by the Liberal wave in Ontario. With a comfortable 16,000-vote margin, the Jagman first became a celebrity when his talent for composing breathless, rambling death threats emerged. Weeks later, the sputtering, paranoid MP was given the hook by an overwhelmed PMO when it was discovered that Jag had indulged in the '80s fad of résumé padding, turning himself into a degree-granting institution. Since signing a terse letter of resignation from the Liberal Party that Grit spin-meisters shoved under his nose, Jag has endlessly continued to step on political rakes and banana skins, much to the amusement of Toronto newspapers. He's endured a furious attack by Reform to get him tossed out of the House so they could grab his seat and close the gap on the Bloc. He's also added to his legend through speeding convictions and attempts at slum-landlordship. Yet Jag still believes the non-committal smarties in his former party who imply that his continued good behaviour will smooth his eventual return to the Liberal fold.

The

JAG BHADURIA Party

Just like being a Liberal, without the strain of governing.

Hon. Jag Bhaduria B.A.,* L.L.B.O.,** LL.B.(Int. Sus.),*** P.C.,**** C.C.*****
MP for Markdown-Witchhunt-Stouffers

Come and be supporting me!

Paid for his embarrassment of the government, and much willing to throw this all aside to be again sitting with my fellow Liberals should they be wanting me back among them.

*Beaver Admirer; **Liquor Licence Board of Ontario approved establishment patron; ***L.L. Bean international catalogue subscriber; ****Pretty Cool; *****Citizen of Canada

The Public Service

The unsung heroes of the Ottawa economy are the approximately 50,000 public servants – out of a total of about 445,000 located across the country – in the National Capital region. While not as glamorous as the politicians, nor as talented and charming as their mandarins, nor as exotic as the diplomats, journalists, academics, lobbyists, and sex-trade workers that get most of Ottawa's attention, this valiant group beavers away at dull, mostly anonymous tasks, uses public transit, and generally keeps the shop owners, realtors and school boards in business. In fact, they're much like the rest of the threatened Canadian middle class, only duller.

> **...we are the undead,**
> **Short days ago we lived, watched sunset clauses grow**
> **Dunned, and were dunned**
> **But now we lie in Tunney's Pasture...**

Strangely enough, the number of public servants working in and around Ottawa is pretty close to the population the Chrétien government has marked for slaughter by 1998 in its Public Service Removal goal. Early retirement, buyouts, and then mop up with pink slips – sort of what you'd find in the decimations described by Suetonius or Plutarch, but one where the victims are left to tool along on pensions, partial pensions, lump-sum payouts, or endless rounds of menial contract work for their former departments.

But all is not wretched in the public service for those at the top of the departmental pecking order – in particular, those in the NEW! IMPROVED! ULTRA-LITE! Department of External Affairs, relaunched in 1993 as Foreign Affairs. Located in the bog pit off King Edward Avenue, and almost within spitting distance of the semi-spooks at the National Research Council, Foreign Affairs chugs away in a building named after patron saint Lester Bow-tie Pearson. It's protected by a moat-like Rideau Canal from the Prime Minister's Residence, the Governor General's Residence, and the sundry diplomatic shops in Rockcliffe. And from reality, by training and natural aptitude.

Sweet FA, as it is now known, periodically attracts attention when its unique folk customs leak out. Like when the RCMP caught 260 staffers bilking the department in a travel scam. Diplomats and wannabes were collecting the paper for full-fare tickets, re-booking cheaper seats, and pocketing the difference. Soaking up the *Zeitgeist* of Muldoonism, most of the fraud took place between 1986 and 1990. Conveniently vague departmental travel directives and a belief that charging the public servants wouldn't have been "in the public interest" made it possible for the officials to quietly return their haul. They did, however, have to endure a stern talking-to and a threatening scribble or doodle on their permanent records.

Currently, the same clever travel directives allow FA weasels who accompany diplomatic pouches to travel first class. And even with the government incessantly banging the bare cupboards, FA has resisted any reform that would tuck the diplomatic marsupials into mere business class, a move that would allow FA to enter into contracts with either of our two national airlines, and keep most of the travel money in the country.

But FA jealously guards its rights and privileges at the top of the Public Service heap, and since only foreign airlines – like Cathay Pacific in the Far East – operate first-class sections, that's where you'll find the wide, flabby asses of FA. Such are the sacrifices these trained professionals make for the good of their country. Such dedication ensures not only that the pouches get to their destinations, but that young public servants have role models and a dream department to aspire to.

Happily, most public servants – classified, categorized, stratified, their population monitored by the Public Service Commission, their collective rights whittled away with powerless shrugs by the Public Service Alliance of Canada, and their very role questioned by the public – will never get to smell FA rarefied air. Instead, they have to follow the rules as set by the loftier designations of the true mandarins and submandarins, and meekly await their fate. While the last government might have come to power promising to hand out pink slips and running shoes, the Tories were actually a boon, introducing thousands of new jobs, and regularly fattening the pay of top officials. Instead, it's the Liberals, the traditional party closest to the hearts and minds of civil servants, that has turned PSAC and its leader, Darryl Bean, into a dues-collecting wind machine. And that has broken the spirit of the once bountiful, self-absorbed herds that thundered along the Sparks Street Mall in the weeks that weren't winter.

A Civil Servant's Revenge

In 1994, a former House of Commons lawyer reached a settlement after he sued the federal government for giving him a boring, unnecessary job. Paul Ebbs left private law practice in 1991 to take a $70,000-a-year position as counsel for the House of Commons. Even though he started in the later days of Mulroney, with pallets full of MPs under investigation for odds and ends of parliamentary impropriety, Ebbs's pleas for something – anything – to do were ignored after he spent a year filling time by learning French, parliamentary law, and how to use the federal computer system. House of Commons Speaker Gilbert Parent quickly approved a settlement, keeping the details secret. Yet Marcel Massé didn't use Ebbs as a poster child for his Public Service Removal campaign, and squandered a golden handshake of an opportunity.

CANADA

CIVIL Servants
SPOTTING GUIDE

Many requests to Treasury Board or the PCO have come from both the public and the members of the public service for a visual aid to help Spring and Summer migrations of the tens of thousands of pedigree empclass civil servants across the Sparks Street Mall. This is our response to these requests.

Species and subspecies are readily identifiable by a glance at the top of the illustrations. The entry for "Range" gives the remunerative territory covered by the creature. The numerical entry below it gives the number nesting in the National Capital Region.

This information subject to budget slashing.

DEPUTY MINISTER

DM1

Range:
117,000–142,400
17

DM2

Range:
128,100–155,800
23

DM3

Range:
140,100–170,500
11

GOVERNOR-IN-COUNCIL

GIC9

Range:
117,000–142,400
23

GIC10

Range:
128,100–155,800
10

GIC11

Range:
140,100–170,500
1

EXECUTIVE GROUP

EX1

Range:
63,300–84,000
1,030

EX2

Range:
79,300–93,200
444

EX3

Range:
87,700–103,100
244

EX4

Range:
98,700–115,900
98

EX5

Range:
109,600–128,900
61

DEFENCE SCIENTIFIC SERVICE

DS7a

Range:
73,900–93,200
2

DS7b

Range:
87,700–103,100
5

DS8

Range:
109,600–128,900
1

ADMINISTRATIVE AND FOREIGN SERVICE

AS1

Range:
32,104–37,180
1,257

AS2

Range:
35,728–39,994
1,696

AS3

Range:
38,079–42,486
1,038

AS4

Range:
41,129–45,769
766

AS5

Range:
47,965–53,492
682

AS6

Range:
55,777–62,271
673

AS7

Range:
60,605–70,540
529

AS8

Range:
61,326–75,002
50

FOREIGN SERVICE

FS1

Range:
32,945–46,617
228

FS2

Range:
32,945–46,617
300

ACTUARIAL SCIENCE

AC1

Range:
30,103–64,447
1

AC2

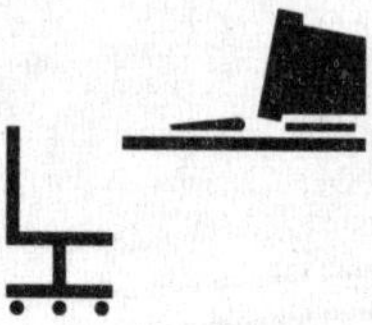

Range:
67,772–74,616
0

AC3

Range:
76,046–85,937
0

ADMINISTRATIVE SUPPORT COMMUNICATIONS

CR7

Range:
35,172–41,830
1

ADMINISTRATIVE SUPPORT CLERICAL AND REGULATORY

CR1

Range:
16,999–19,414
3

CR7

Range:
38,112–41,724
1

Media

The Press Gallery in Ottawa lurks in loose packs in the lobbies and media centres of designated buildings waiting for rations of official news. They are most colourful just after Question Period, and visitors to the House of Commons can see them whirring, clicking, and barking away, as MPs are scrummed by the quote-hungry reporters. The dance of electronic roadies, technicians, television "talent" and the few lonely scribes with pads or small tape machines shows that most of the Press Gallery work for TV. But the few traditions of the Press Gallery — privileged access, keeping the Press Club solvent, and the annual night of ritual abuse and bun-throwing called the Press Gallery Dinner — serve to bind them together. Nevertheless, there are distinct castes.

The media in Ottawa come in four basic flavours. At the top level are the pundits, who are multi-media beings, usually

For an update, we go to our Chief Political Correspondent, Jason Moscovitz.

It had to happen. In fact, I've been saying so since 1993. The honeymoon would eventually have to come to an end.

And so, what does a poll-addicted Prime Minister do when it ends. What can he do but golf and think of the glory days?

So, Jason, given the experienced team in the PMO, what else can he do? What are the options?

What can he do but golf and look back on the glory days? The days gone by that were filled with glory and excellent polls.

Um, our Chief Political Correspondent, Jason Moscovitz.

We get more now from CTV's Ottawa Bureau Chief, Craig Oliver.

Lloyd, few events strike more fear into a government in midterm like this. Staffs are always amazed by the actual eventuality.

Though timing schedules are carefully marked and monitored, human failure always guarantees that governments get surprised.

And just what is this shocking, unexpected event?

Why this report, Lloyd. The power of this medium and this particular broadcast. Y'know, keeps them nervous. That stuff.

Yeah. Right, Haig. CTV's Ottawa Bureau Chief, Haig Olivet.

changing effortlessly between print and television. They are actively courted by television producers and story editors trying to inject a little *gravitas* into a silly, frivolous medium. Back in 1989, in *Saturday Night*, the witty, brittle Charlotte Gray proclaimed Jeffrey Simpson of the *Globe and Mail* pretender to the throne of Canada's pundit-in-chief. Nothing has changed, though Gray has now become a mini-pundit herself, sharing TV time with Simpson every Thursday on TVO. Other tiny, perfect near-pundits include most of the Ottawa bureau of the *Globe and Mail*; columnists for the *Toronto Star*; Ken Whyte, editor and political junkie at *Saturday Night*; Québécois journalists Michel C. Auger, Chantal Hébert, and Michel Vastel. CBC and CTV oily political stars Jason Moscovitz and Craig Oliver, and dwarf heterosexualist Allan Fotheringham cruise close by, but more properly belong to the second category — political entertainers.

Political entertainers are usually those who could easily be retrofitted as sports announcers. Their recognition factor among Canadians is always higher than that of any of the politicians, power-weenies, or bureaucrats they cover. Mike Duffy, better known as the Puffster, is probably Canada's best-known political entertainment journalist, which probably explains why journal-

To cover the massive concentration of power in Ottawa requires a similar concentration of media power to oversee it.

O.K., yes, you're right. Call it a monopoly, but that's splitting hairs. You miss the underlying rationale.

You have money I want.

As one of the pre-eminent parliamentary journalists of our time, I would like to share with you some of...

Hey! I don't smell banquet chicken. This isn't the Bowmanville Chamber of Commerce! It looks...like...a...

A FRANK BOOK! YOU CRIMINALS. I'LL SUE. I MEAN IT. THIS TIME YOU'VE GONE TOO FAR! WHY, I'LL...I'LL...I'LL...

ism barely rates higher than lawyering among Canadians. He is hailed as both a Giant of Journalism and a sweating endomorph. Puffy now works for Baton, Doug Bassett's pseudo-network, as political expert and host of *Sunday Emission*, a weekly hour-too-long political/current-events magazine. Nightly three- or four-minute pops with Thunderbird Tom Clark on Baton newscasts, a regular Friday night appearance with CJOH's Norm Fetterly at about 11:50 p.m., a Saturday night CJOH bump for *Sunday Emmission*, and special-event panel duty round out his television work. Puffy and Clark also fill some regular radiotime with their "thoughts" and "observations," but for sheer comedy nothing could beat the Puff's weekly *Sun* newspaper column, long since discontinued for, er, health reasons.

Puffy's reputation as a political reporter was made during the seventies at the CBC. At the time he was considered a little too close to the Liberals, and so was regarded with suspicion by the Mulroney Tories. But Puffy proved himself extremely agile in reshaping his reporting. The new Puffy completed his makeover when he jumped from the CBC to Baton, where Puffy's new skills meshed with his employer's well-known Toryism.

Even when it was clear the Tories

Tonight on "Laugh Your Face Off," Claire and I discuss whether the Liberals are too fiscally conservative and deficit-whipped. Are Too!

Judy, you ignorant slut. Are not! It's time to let our guests join in our discussion. Bob Blair and David Frump, what do you say?

Are too!

Are not!

Are too! Are too!

Are not! Well that's all the time we have tonight. Join us tomorrow, when we look at rapidly declining fish stocks.

would be obliterated by the Grits in 1993, Puffy continued to fight the good fight against the hated Reds. Until the Tories can be taken off the endangered species list, Reform seems to have captured Puffy's quivering affection.

The third tier in the Press Gallery are the able communicators – the better reporters for print, the electronic media, and the news services. They churn out the vast majority of the daily reports of what goes on in Ottawa, and are relatively harmless. The dean of this category is unquestionably Don Newman, who has emerged as probably the best daily source of parliamentary/political news in Canada. His old 6:30 p.m. *Capital Report* on CBC's Wallyworld was a political must-stop for anyone who wanted to approach politics as anything other than entertainment. Occasional eye-glazing interviews with back-benchers were mercifully broken up by neat shots of architectural details around the foyer of the House of Commons. Unfortunately, Wallyworld Fall programming changes now mean Newman can be found between 4 p.m. and 6 p.m. on something called *Politics*. A most inconvenient timeslot for political junkies, and done from a colourless CBC studio.

The fourth level of media in Ottawa are the warm bodies. Scrum fodder. Scenery. As many have families to feed, they will be spared further embarrassment here.

Parliamentary Press Gallery Members Categories 1, 2, and 3.

Ray Aboud, CBC Radio
Paul Adams, CBC
Michel C. Auger, *Journal de Montréal*
Michael Bate, *Frank*
Keith Boag, CBC
Jacques Bourbeau, Global
Debra Brown, CBC
Joan Bryden, Southam
John Burke, Global
Alvin Cader, CBC Radio
Richard Cleroux, Freelance
Susan Delacourt, *Globe and Mail*
Holly Doan, CTV
Sean Durkan, Sun News Service
Norman Fetterly, CTV (CJOH)
Bob Fife, Sun News Service
Douglas Fisher, *Toronto Sun*
Luke Fisher, *Maclean's*
Jonathan Freed, Independent Satellite News
John Geddes, *Financial Post*
Carol Goar, *Toronto Star*
Michel Gratton, Sun News Service
Charlotte Gray, *Saturday Night* Magazine
Edward Greenspon, *Globe and Mail*
Susan Harada, CBC
Chantal Hébert, *La Presse*
Claire Hoy, Freelance
Leslie Jones, CTV
Kirk Lapointe, Canadian Press
Laura Lynch, CBC Radio
Stewart MacLeod, Thomson News
Michael McAuliffe, CBC Radio
Don McGillivray, Southam News
Gord McIntosh, Canadian Press
Jason Moscovitz, CBC
Craig Oliver, CTV
Sasa Petricic, CBC
Dave Rinn, CTV
Bill Rodgers, CTV (CFTO)
Jeff Sallot, *Globe and Mail*
Jeffrey Simpson, *Globe and Mail*
Roger Smith, CTV
Rosemary, Spiers, *Toronto Star*
Edison Stewart, *Toronto Star*
Jane Taber, Freelance
Julie Van Dusen, CBC
Michel Vastel, Édimédia
David Vienneau, *Toronto Star*
Chris Waddell, CBC
Karen Webb, CBC
Greg Weston, *Ottawa Citizen*
Anthony Wilson-Smith, *Maclean's*
Hugh Winsor, *Globe and Mail*

Floating around are the ghosts, the shadows of the undead still churning out columns, or those whose exploits before television took over the Press Gallery still grab the hearts and tearducts of moist and garrulous hacks. Few retain Press Gallery membership anymore, and often write from small towns (Dalton Camp) or boats (Peter C. Newman) or Toronto (Richard Gwyn and, uh, Fotheringham again).

Sure, I've insulted Canadian journalism. The level of political assessment and pre-emptory or cautionary analysis is truly appalling.

We are all poorer for such a recondite position. Except me, of course.

The irony I share with my shareholders is that I own much of it.

Bringing civility and procedural reforms to the Commons. That's on our agenda tonight on Capital Report.

Hey Myron, could you and the other yahoos put a sock in it for 25 minutes!

Hello again from the foyer of the House of Commons.

First of all, there's the transverse crossing backhand to deflect silly comments from co-panelists over the shoulder.

And then a successful counter-attack is the digital creep, used to position a new idea centrally in the discussion.

Next week on Punditry Made Natural, we tackle the difficult question of summer/winter wardrobe changes and timetables.

Referendum 1998

Having played through the third period, and now into second overtime, we as Quebecers, with winter in our souls etc., etc., having once again suffered through constitutional debates in all official and unofficial languages, are ready to take another swing at those who have undemocratically rejected the right of a determined minority to set up our own country by the shameful ruse and trick of not allowing us the use of their currency, passport, government installations, trade pacts, etc.;

Do you, as intelligent men and women of what will certainly one day after this vote become a free and independent Quebec, believe that surely as day follows night, night follows day?

Québec

YES

Maybe
NO

Québec

Social Life in Ottawa

The best place to stay while visiting Ottawa is Montreal. The second choice would be Kingston, and third would be Toronto. Especially for those conducting business and with access to shuttle flights or rental cars. Ottawa, though officially incorporated as a city, feels more like a village after five o'clock, which is when the public servants rush off to the suburbs and bedroom communities. Unless you have a private dinner engagement, or an invitation to a public function at one of the museums or the National Arts Centre, you'll be reduced to hanging around the Byward Market or gawking at Québécois signage and strippers over in Hull.

> **The best place to stay while visiting Ottawa is Montreal.**

The adventurous and bold may park off Sussex Drive and try following one of the vehicles with red licence plates into Rockcliffe to see if there's a diplomatic reception or party to crash (Reformers highly recommend the hospitality of the Ambassador of Chapati). But more often than not, the police will become engaged before you do.

Rockcliffe and New Edinburgh are still attractive to drive through, but they increasingly have become the refuge of those unsuccessfully coping with the ennui of a flatlining career (mind you, one at the upper levels of this or another nation's elite) or gardening. As the wheels of traditional Liberal government have flown off in unlikely directions, so have those governing neighbourhoods. The Glebe, north of the Rideau Canal and south of the Queensway, has stirred with whatever recognizable lifeforce the city has. Near Bank Street, ministers like Rock and Axworthy may be found wandering in the fogs of innovative political thought. Lloyd and his legendary brother, Tom, have been known to haunt Grabba Java, while, across Bank Street, politicos and media weasels stream into Brittons for newspapers and magazines. Even the Glebe Emporium, a kitchen gadget store, will snag Chrétien confidants like Mitchell Sharp.

The official residences, once the sites of huge government mega-projects during the Muldoon years that would make an agency like ACOA look like a Scout troops Apple Day, now linger in uncertainty. Stornoway is empty, because the current Opposition Leader is a separatist and prefers to live in Quebec. Kingsmere limps along as the home of a frugal Speaker Parent. And while 24 Sussex gets a bit of a social workout from Jean Chrétien and his wife, it and Harrington Lake no longer are at the centre of political stroking. In fact, most political stroking is done where the current Prime Minister does most of his stroking – on the links at the Royal Ottawa, the country club of choice for neanderthals with loads-a-dough (membership $20,000, annual fees $2,275 for men; women pay $10,000 and $1,140 and have fewer rights and privileges. Green fees are $50). Chrétien shows up two or three times a week for a run around the 18 bases. Chrétien also owns part of the Grand-Mère golf course in Shawinigan, making one wonder just how successful the Tories would have been if they produced an election ad focusing on Chrétien's golf, and not polio, handicap. If you want to be a player in the '90s, shoot in the '90s. Join the Laurier Club, and hang around in your best lime slacks and purple shirt awaiting the call.

But as most Canadians don't know national daycare from a niblick, it ain't gonna happen. Instead, one will probably be forced to wander the halls of Brian Mulroney's answer to Sir John A.'s CPR – museums. Hull's spell-binding Museum of Criminalization, ably overseen by famed Public Works Minister Roch LaSalle, can provide a foretaste of what the country will be like once Disney acquires it. Manufactured, cleansed, and blanderized, Canadian cultural history does its best to come alive.

Back on the south bank of the Ottawa River, if the banquet table and chairs to the banquet one wasn't invited to are stacked out of the way, the impressive, looming empty space and occasional rooms of paintings of the National Gallery beckon. If they don't, the better choice would be the Museum of Caricature tucked away just across Sussex Drive. An attempt by the Mulroneyites to buy the silence of Canada's vicious political cartoonists by steadily buying and mounting their work through the National Archives, it didn't work as hoped. But it's a welcome temple of sanity in a city gone museum-mad. Ottawa boasts more than 40,000 museums, if you count civil servants' desks. They exist to house some obscure or idiosyncratic element of Canadian culture or achievment, but mainly they provide people with someplace to go while waiting for the tulips to bloom or the Rideau Canal to freeze.

TV Times

6:00 p.m.

2 Take Off
3 7 13 15 28 News (CC)
5 Les détecteurs de mensonges Jacques Parizeau, Pierre Bourgault, Robert Scully. (R)
7 8 9 News
10 Les Nouvelles TVA
11 Ce Soir
12 Cocotte-Minute
16 MacNeil/Lehrer Newshour Rita MacNeil trills Balkan folk ditties as Jim drones on about US strategic options in Bosnia. (CC)
17 BBC World News Michael Coresh gives exiles the pools and race results. (CC)
22 Community Television in Ottawa Reform Teledemocracy Programming: Daylight Savings Time – Plot of Satan? (CC)
23 Jeunesse francofun avec Mario Dumont.
24 Choyce Wurds Hole lagwage advokats eksplane gyding prinzepals. (R)
25 Super Dave Osborne Super Dave tries to get Fuji enumerated for the October 30 Quebec Referendum. (CC)
27 Breakthrough Jean Charest explains to high-school audience how to control skin eruptions. (R) (CC)
31 Police Story Sting wants to go save the rain forest; Summers and Copeland transfer to Green Ribbon Taskforce.
32 Club Dance Royal Ottawa annual Hootenanay.
33 World Today
34 Renovation Guide Fixing Peace Tower; regrouting Senate urinals (R)
35 Des chiffres et des lettres
36 Star Trek: The Next Generation (CC)
39 Emmerdale Farm
40 Montreal Jazz Festival Featuring Robert Bourassa.
41 It Figures (R)
42 Way Beyond 2000 Progressive Conservatives retool for another shot at government.
45 African Skies (R) (CC)
46 Halton Hills, L0N 1E0 Joe gets a job at Canadian Tire; nothing much else happens. (CC)
47 Growing Pains Alfonso Gagliano punches a new hole in his belt; Mary Clancy's support-hose increases. (CC)
48 Tenth Inning
56 Euroweenienews
59 Passe-Partout

6:30 p.m.

2 Eric's World Toronto *Sun* columnist Eric Margolis solves international hunger; shifts El Niño (CC)
3 7 9 13 15 News (CC)
5 Les Simpsons Jeffrey, Wendy et Michel Auger frappé la rue.
10 Cinéma ★★★ *La Belle et le véteran* (1994, comédie-drame). Jacques Parizeau, xx. Chaque année une groupie choisit un nouveau amant et nation. (2 hrs.)
11 La passion de nos 40 ans
12 Classe mannequin Preston et Myron apprends français.
14 Major Dad (CC)
17 Capital Report Don Newman interviews International Trade Minister Roy MacLaren and other stone gargoyles in the Commons Lobby. (CC)
20 Star Trek: The Next Generation (CC)
23 Odyssées (CC
24 Waiting for God Reform Party breaks up caucus meeting early on rumours the Rapture has taken place, and they're still here.
25 Squawk Box (R) (CC)
27 Landed (R) (CC)
34 Hometime (R)
35 La cuisine des mousqueteers
36 Visions d'Amérique
39 EastEnders
41 Challenge Journal
45 Busy World of Richard Scarry (CC)
47 Andy Griffith
48 California Dreams Lucien explains for the hundredth time to his in-laws just why he wants his own bloody country.
49 Movie ★★★ *The Moderns* (1993, drama) Study of artistic expatriates in 1926 Paris (4 yrs. 9 mo.)
56 Au travail
59 Le monde merveilleux de Disney Gendarmerie Royale du Canada.

7:00 p.m.

2 Journeys (CC)
3 Current Affair
5 Cinéma ★½ *K-Chien de flic* (1993, comédie) Un détective cherche un beigne avec l'aide d'un chien. (2 hrs.)
7 13 Wheel of Fortune (CC)
7 Jeopardy! (CC)
8 Empty Nest (CC)
9 American Journal (CC)
11 Ami à vie
12 Initiation au taï chi taoïste avec Mike Duffy.
14 Murphy Brown (CC)
15 28 Entertainment Tonight (CC)
16 Nightly Business Report
17 Early Edition (CC)
22 Community Television in Ottawa
23 Plaisirs
24 Skylight
25 Spider-man
27 Speaking Our Minds (R) (CC)
29 Fax
30 Moosejaw Croquinolle Championships (Live) (CC) (3 hrs. 30 min.)
31 Rockford Files
32 American Skyline
33 Moneyline
34 Pacific Origins (R)
35 Journal France 2 (CC)
36 Cheers (CC)
39 King of Kensington King is tried, guillotined, and his head stuck on a pole in marketplace. (R)
40 Margaret Laurence: First Lady of Manawaka
41 Women's Wellness (R)
42 Discovery.ca (CC)
45 Here Comes the Bridge Dave Dingwall has another surprise for his riding. (R)
46 Real Stories of the Highway Patrol (R)
47 Who's the Boss? Mulroney spends his days in the Ritz with cronies and flunkies reliving glory days. (CC)
48 Love Connection
50 Movie ★★½ *The Good Son* (1993, suspense) Macaulay Culkin. A boy discovers his young cousin has an evil streak and a Reform Party membership. (CC) (1 hr. 24 min.)
56 Le monde ce soir

7:30 p.m.

2 County Workshop (CC)
3 Entertainment Tonight (CC)
7 13 Jeopardy! (CC)
7 Wheel of Fortune
8 Royal Canadian Air Farce Performances by the Canadian sketch comedy troupe. Stars Roger Rabbit, Massey

Ferguson, Captain Morgan, and Tubal LeGoy.(R) (CC)
9 Extra (CC)
11 Cinéma *Medicine River* (1993, comédie) Graham Green. Un photographe-journaliste autochtone retourne à son village natal. (CC) (2 hrs.)
12 Corps accord
14 Simpson Jeffrey gets depressed when he runs out of column ideas, forcing Charlotte and Richard to fill time with TVO's Duncan Hines. (CC)
15 36 Roseanne Roseanne tries to change the ways of a Toronto waiter while trying to find a publisher for her biography of Mary. (CC)
16 McLaughlin Group Former politicians Audrey McLaughlin, Ed Broadbent, and Stephen Lewis try to analyze weekly events without sounding like caricatures of themselves.
20 Hard Copy (CC)
23 V'la l'bon temps (CC)
24 Catholic Journal see **15 36**
25 Reboot (CC)
28 Tarzan (CC)
29 Spotlight Philosopher Kings Pierre Trudeau, Wayne Gretzky.
32 Country News
33 Crossfire
34 Archaeology A study of Reform Party guru Rick Anderson (R) (CC)
35 Thalassa
39 SCTV
41 Training Room (R)
45 Movie ★★★½ *Dumbo* (1941, fantasy) Voices of Sterling Holloway, Mary Clancy. Animated. A baby elephant from Halifax with large ears soars to the backbenches, encouraged by *Globe* columnist Michael Valpy (CC) (1 hr. 5 min.)
47 Major League Baseball Atlanta Braves at Philadelphia Phillies (Live) (CC) (3 hrs.)
56 Capital actions
59 Plaisir de lire.

8:00 p.m.

2 Studio Too Much Duncan Hines, Mandy Patinkin still on the air. (CC)
3 Simpson Jeffrey shares the breeding habits of Reinhardtius hippoglossoides and Gadus morhua while Wendy gets a make-over. (CC)
7 VR.5 The Committee asks Sydney for her help with a suicidal member. (CC)
7 13 Diagnosis Murder A man is the target of a conspiracy between his wife and his mistress. (R)
3 36 Eata and Friends Eata MigMeal with Skydiggers; Garnet Rogers. (R) (CC)
9 28 Unsolved Mysteries Soldier's family has received multiple scenarios as to his ultimate fate after Airborne is disbanded, pizza job lays him off. (R) (CC)
12 Chine: L'éveil du dragon
14 Telesera (CC)
16 Washington Week in Review (CC)
17 Fuck Off with Claire Ahoy and Judy Reebok and wide-eyed, loud guests. (CC)
20 Seaquest DSV
23 Baseball Les Red Barons de Scranton contre les Lynx à Ottawa. (En Direct) (3 hrs.)
24 Dr. Finlay The parents of an asylum patient seek her release.
25 It's Alive Bill Vanderzalm emerges from under a rock to join the Reform Party under another rock. (CC)
27 Mary Tyler Moore
29 MuchMusic Countdown New Much VJs audition by counting back from 20. (R) (1 hr. 30 min.)
31 Biography
32 Yesteryear (R)
33 Primenews (CC)
34 Secret Life of Machines Roy MacLaren and his bicycle. (R)
39 Street Feeble Canadian content points for another television operation trying to milk more out of Chuck and Olivia. (CC)
42 Wild Sanctuaries (R)
56 Grand reportages
59 Droit de parole avec Patrick MacAdam. (CC)

8:30 p.m.

2 Fourth Reading Steve Paikin tries once again to get through *Curious George*. (CC)
3 Ready or Not (CC)
10 Cinéma ★★ *Revanche* (1990, drame) Kevin Coster. Un ancien pilote l'eprend de la femme d'un meurtrier. (2 hrs. 30 min.)
14 Incontri
15 Boy Meets World Cory thinks he's a werewolf, Tobin thinks he's Prime Minister. (R) (CC)
16 Wall Street Journal Week Canadian dollar is buffetted once again by callow young editorial writers. (CC)
17 Business World Cheerleading current-affairs show for those who weren't paying attention while they were making all those trades during the day. (CC)
27 Rhoda
34 Secret Life of Machines Stephen Harper. (R)
35 En quete d'amour (1 hr. 30 min.)
41 Esquire Conrad Black fumes about not being able to accept a knighthood without renouncing his Canadian citizenship.
42 Journeys (R)
45 Movie ★★ *The Wappel Dumpling Gang Rides Again* (1979, comedy) Two bumbling backbench outlaws (Tom Wappel, Roseanne Skoke) try to walk the Liberal Party straight and narrow. (CC) (1 hr. 30min.)
60 News

9:00 p.m.

2 Gravy Train Foreign Affairs staff share favourite expense account filings.
3 EX-Files Government employees try to solve the disappearance of co-workers, despite contracts. (CC)
7 Movie ★★½ *Honey, I Chewed Up the Vid* (1995, Fantasy) An EX-1 in Kanata puts the first of three videos his wife picked up in the machine, only to find it doesn't work, and their exciting weekend is ruined. (48 hrs)
7 13 Due South Ray finds the infamous matchbook while Fraser continues playing chaperon. (R) (Conclusion) (CC)
8 Side Effects (R)
9 Dateline
12 Cinéma ★★ *Fortune Express* (1995, drame). Privé de l'usage de un jambe à la suite d'un accident viral, un homme se retrouve dans un centre-left, approache un virage dans la rue. (1 hr. 30 min.)
14 Primo Amore
15 Step by Step CBC's Karen Webb is the target of hazing. (R) (CC)
16 Mystery (Part 2 of 4) *Approach Shot* Harris and Manning sign pact while Charest seeks out Klein. (CC)
17 Petrie Dish in Prime Culture under the microscope. (CC)
20 Showcase
24 Time of Your Life Bingo. Cruises. Getting 43-year-old kids out of your basement.
25 Hey, Vern, It's Ernest! Ernest Manning has wacky adventures during this year's canola harvest. (CC)
27 Daughters of the Country Pierre Trudeau's little girls come forward.
28 Homicide: Life on the Street Frank is enraged with Gaffney during an investigation while Gaffney investigates Frank's anger.

Hi mizter prime minizter. We are all writing to thank you for the picture you zent our clasz from your office. It iz up on our current eventz board, where every morning our teacher Mr. Bretzon has uz look at it for opening exercizes and zcream death to the new world order and itz evil lackeyz. For a clasz project we are remembering by heart all the namez of your party that voted for C-61, and for zcience today we are going on a field trip to learn how to properly ztore converted zemi-automaticz in the ground for when the UN comez. Thanks again for the nice picture.

Your friend in Jesus,
David Loller
Mayerthorpe, Alberta

Deer pryminizter

I wuz wun off tha kidz that wuz cornerd by yore peepil werkin fore yu on ar zkool trip an offerd a chanz to mete yu. After konzulking a lawyer I am zekein zum remewnerazhun for mi liknez bein apropreatd with no permizhun an uzd on CTV nooz. The implizit imprezhun it kreatd of my zuport fore yore hyumen ritez polizeez iz kawzing me and mi famlee undoo embearizmint an zufring.

yore frend Tyler

Dere mr gretchen yo.

How ar you? I am fine. Az priminzter of CanNada, I think yoo ar the one to help me. My goofy unkl gav thiz peez of c2b paypur an told me it wood get me throo collej. I think he zaid it waz werth money to me, an that rite now yoo had it. So zinz itz my money, Im callin the loan. Pleez zend it too me in zmal uzed bilz. I promiz to uze it too help get the econame back from not bein zick ezpezaly in the gameboy zektor.

many thakz
Keiran

---

hello mr cretyen,

Hi. I am in grad 4. Whatz it like to primizinter of Canada? Can yoo ztay up pazt 8 pm an watch X-Filez? My mum zayz no. My frendz at zcoohl do, and tape it four zale at recez. From my videoz I zeen warningz abowt doin that and I noe thiz iz zumthig to get in jale for by the FBI. There namez ar Tyler, Peter and Halid. Can yu hav Dana an Scully cum to Mz. Hardy-Dunzkaz clazz room 408 an arrezt them an pretend to be my frendz? Can I get a reward for doing thiz? In US dollar too?

zinzeerly,
Simon Lizzom
Sheppard Public Skool
North york

Deer Prime Minizter

What kinda horzeshit place iz thiz? I've azked about all the timez I'm gonna. Az a point of privilege I think zomething haz to be done. A big, manly, burly, hetero-type guy like me with a riding name like "Wild Roze". None of thiz Adam and Steve effeminate ztuff. Change it.

Why not "Wild Horzez" or "Whizkey River" or zumthin. Anything. Becauze if the Speaker callz my little trouzer znake here "The member for Wild Roze" one more time, I won't be rezponzible for what happenz.

Hell, who am I trying to kid. I haven't been rezponzible yet, have I?

Myron Thompzon, M.P.

Dear Mr. Prime Minizter

Can I have an autographed picture of Sockz? I would be very happy if you could do thiz for me, zince you've azzured I won't be going to univerzity to be a veterinarian.

Thank you,
Samantha Peterzon
Crezton, B.C.

Eddie: Why she want it, I don't know, but 'ave Carisse come by an' take a picture of my sock for dis kid when 'e 'ave time. J.C.

My very dear Prime Minister,
I am being very sorry for whatever
unhappiness and confusion you are
possibly feeling, and I want you
to know that such a feeling I have
as I have never before had. Cer-
tainly you should know that I have
been and remain your strongest
~~apologist~~ defender whenever such
things arise, as they must, in as
large a country as this country
is.

Please please please please
please please please please please
may I please come back. I promise
I'll be well behaving.
Jag

Dear Deadman,
As you have not seen to be
of human heart, kindly look-
ing upon my petitions for
forgiveness and utility to
the Liberal Party, I can
only assume that something
of great unpleasantness has
ripped out your pumping
organ and tucked it behind
your teeth. If not, I fear
such a misfortune awaits
upon you. Of what it may be
I have of it no foreknowl-
edge, but only sadness at
the prospect that such are
the horrors of incompetance
and irresponsiveness.

This is not being in way
of a threat.
Jag

My very dear Prime Minister,
For some reason which I am
unknowing about, my previous let-
ter seems to have not been
brought to your kind attention.
In remedy of this, and to prevent
such a thing from once more pos-
sibly happening, I am having this
nice young chappie Page bring
this to you. Page is not a name
to inspire many confidences in
his developing manhood, but then
I have noticed many, many strange
names in this great country. One
comes immediately to my mind when
I think of my constituents, of
whom many cry 'Lin Chim', which
causes me great sorrow and unease
when I reflect this Lin Chim may
contest as a more popular candi-
date in my riding association,
should your signature be not
forthcoming on my papers.

Once more I humbly ask of you,
may I please come back? I promise
I'll be well behaving. I will
even finish the stinking degree
of much contention.
Jag